THE HEALTHY ALTERNATIVE:
NATURALLY
YOURS GOURMET
DESSERTS

Yvonne Sanders-Butler Ed.D.

For additional information and ordering books, contact:
Naturally Yours and More Inc.
P.O. Box 892
Ellenwood, Georgia 30294
www.ybnatural.com

First edition. July 2002
Printed in Canada

ISBN 0-9720362-0-2

Library of Congress Control Number: 2002092149

Please consult your physician before using recipes in this book if you have medical restrictions. This book does not take the place of a prescribed diet by your physician. Do not substitute any of the recipes for a medically prescribed diet.
The author is not a medical physician. The information provided is from personal experiences and the author's research.

CONTENTS

DEDICATION

This book is dedicated to my brother, Johnathan "Man" Sanders. You inspired me in life and in death. You have taught me to never take life for granted. Because of you I know that dreams really do come true. I miss you and I love you.

To my Uncle, Shepherd Waters, who turned all of his challenges into opportunities. You taught me early in life to appreciate differences. You were my first friend. I miss you and I love you.

FOREWORD

Good news!!! Yvonne Butler's compilation of recipes in "Naturally Yours Gourmet Desserts" provides us with a second chance to capture some of those forgotten recipes. Not only are recipes included for coconut cake and custard pie, but her Mom's Choice section includes snacks that children will enjoy. Recently, at a school fundraiser, Dr. Butler prepared the smorgasbord dessert table with many delectable goodies from Naturally Yours Gourmet Desserts. Needless to say, since I arrived late, the parents only left cheesecake crumbs.

Let's face it. Many of us need to modify our eating behavior and increase physical activity. There are a variety of nutrition resources to help in this process such as the Food Guide Pyramid and The Dietary Guidelines for Americans. Desserts and pastries are some of the major food items in many diets that we are told have to be eliminated. But not so with Naturally Yours Gourmet Desserts which includes a nutrient analysis with the amounts of servings for all recipes. Many of these recipes include soy products, and a reduced amount of sugar, sodium, and fat. With careful planning and checking with your dietitian and physician, you can still include these occasionally in your meal plan. Remember make meal pattern changes gradually, watch your serving size, increase your activity, and drink plenty of water. Maximize the future for the next generation! Take care of your temple and enjoy the wonderful recipes in Naturally Yours Gourmet Desserts.

Lorine Phillips Bizzell, R.D., M.S., MBA

INTRODUCTION

I never intended to write a book, instead, I intended to try to overcome some personal health challenges in my life, and, through this process, "Naturally Yours Gourmet Desserts" was born. It has been a very spiritual journey for me. One that has made me cry and laugh, and one that has given me renewed respect for life and living.

First, this is not a diet book. Rather, it promotes healthy eating which is unique when it comes to sweets. I now know that instead of opening and closing my refrigerator all day, I must have a well-balanced diet and appropriate physical activity to improve my health and lose weight.

After 23 years of unsuccessful dieting, I have realized that commercial diets are too faddish and unhealthy for the majority of people like me, and diet pills can kill you. I also know that after many years of unsuccessful dieting, behavior modification is crucial for me to obtain a successful lifestyle change and to improve my overall health. To me, this meant eliminating laxatives, diuretics, and diet pills from my medicine closet that used to give me a quick fix.

I could no longer continue to waste money to rejoin diet programs that did not work. I could no longer look at the television for hours to find the miracle diet that did not exist. I could no longer buy every new diet book that hit the bookstands that suggested "eat all you want and lose weight." Last but not least, I had to overcome the compulsion to secretly look for doctors who would prescribe the ultimate diet drug, for me even if pre-existing health conditions did not allow me to use the drug.

One of my biggest fears was when I used the diet drugs, Phen-phen and Redux. I never told my husband or family because I was the only one in my family who ever took diet drugs. I didn't want them to tell me that I could do it on my own and that diet drugs were bad for me. Well, after I had been on the drug Phen-phen for about six months, a report was published stating that the drug was killing people. As a result, it was removed from the market. I was terrified! Not only did I feel that I would probably die, but the doctor who prescribed the drugs for me would not return my phone calls. I later learned that she had left the business. How would I explain to everyone that a very educated and intelligent woman could do something so stupid? What I can tell you is that when one feels desperate, one will do anything. Never place yourself in such a vulnerable position. I am blessed because my life was spared. There are many people who lost their lives in their quest to be healthy or to just feel normal. My heart goes out to their children and families. Perhaps my life has been spared to share my story with you.

More than 10 years ago I was diagnosed with hypertension and sarcoidosis, a chronic disease in the lupus family that affected my lungs and also caused me to experience severe arthritic symptoms. My physician suggested I lose 50 pounds to take the pressure off of my weakened joints, which I already knew. I became depressed because I had no control of my food intake, and it affected every other part of my life. My sisters, who knew that this disease could be fatal if I did not make some immediate changes, were doing research and recommending herbs and physical activity while cheering and encouraging me. It was my sister Betty who informed me of a group that could support me in losing weight without dieting. "This would be a first," I thought. "What did I have to lose?" I began to attend a support group called "Overcomers." Jeanie and Linda, my group leaders, helped me to remain focused.

I was just addicted to certain foods that I loved. After I realized that there were other people who were truly addicted to sugar and foods high in carbohydrates, the healing process started. All of my life I believed that I lacked willpower. It is hard to diet alone, and it is acceptable and wonderful to seek support. Become empowered to make the necessary changes to live healthier or to lose weight. Don't depend on others like I did for over 25 years.

For the past five years I have been involved with and founded a wellness program that offers group support for individuals who are seeking a healthier lifestyle. I know that based on my genetic make-up and environment, what I eat determines my well-being and my weight. I found that when I used natural ingredients to prepare my recipes, I began to lose weight without dieting. After several years of extensive research, I have learned that one can eat all enjoyable foods, especially desserts, if they are properly prepared, without gaining unwanted pounds. The only exception is if one has a prescribed medical condition that dictates otherwise.

Desserts are normally eliminated from one's diet when trying to lose weight or seeking improved health. Well, the good news is that when we prepare our foods using natural ingredients instead of processed ingredients such as enriched flours, white sugars, and dairy products, we get fewer food cravings, fewer digestive problems, and less weight gain.

The recipes in this book have been created with love and compassion for those of us who enjoy desserts, who want to stay healthy, and who do not want to feel guilty about eating our favorite desserts.

Cakes &

THE TIMELESS AROMA OF
MS. RUTH'S SWEETBREAD.

Sweetbread was my first memory of cakes since my mom always made sweetbread for us. I always knew when she was going to make sweetbread. She would take out her ingredients the day before. The following day I would watch her as she carefully placed all the ingredients in a small worn bowl. I do not remember seeing her measure the ingredients with a measuring cup or measuring spoon. My mother quickly mixed all of the ingredients and allowed me to sample the batter before she poured the mixture into an old beaten, tin cake pan. Then she would place it in a big belly black stove that was heated by wood. She normally made one pan of sweetbread and if we had company, she made two pans. Mom only had one pan that she used for baking cakes, so she would wash the pan and reuse it to get

frosting

her second pan of sweetbread. I always knew when the cake was ready because the sweet aroma flowed through every room in our three-room house. Mom removed the cake from the stove and set it on top of the oven to cool.

It was called sweetbread and not cake because she only used self-rising white flour, homemade butter, eggs from the hen house, sugar, flavor and canned milk. She used fewer eggs than when she made a layer cake and she never frosted it. Mom only frosted cakes for special occasions like Easter or Christmas. Until then we were perfectly happy with sweetbread. My mother had several specialty cakes such as caramel cake, coconut cake and chocolate cake. Those were the cakes that Santa liked most. But to us kids, all of mom's cakes were special. I enjoy our cake baking times together now as much as I did when I was three and four years old.

My baking today incorporates my techniques and skills along with those of my mother and my ancestors who I have admired and respected over the years. It has also embraced the techniques and skills of those who have introduced us to non-traditional yet great desserts from the vegetarian community. Many of the people who had such a profound effect on my cake baking will not see this book become a reality. But I know it was their preparation, hard work and sacrifice over the years that have given me the energy and spirit to move forward in my lifestyle change to create "Naturally Yours Gourmet Desserts." I owe such a great debt of gratitude to these women. It has been a great journey.

HEAVENLY CHOCOLATE CAKE

1 1/2 cups unbleached, all-purpose white flour
1 cup oat flour
1/2 cup Dutch-processed cocoa
1 1/2 teaspoons baking powder
1 teaspoon baking soda
1 tablespoon apple cider vinegar
2 teaspoons vanilla extract
1 teaspoon lemon extract
1 cup cold water
4 organic eggs
1 cup soy butter, cut in pats and melted in
the microwave for approximately 35 seconds, see note
1 1/2 cups natural sugar
1/2 cup soymilk

Preheat oven to 350 degrees. Sift flour twice, sifting unbleached flour and oat flours together the first time. For the second sifting, combine flours, sugar, cocoa, baking powder, and baking soda; set aside. Use whisk to blend milk, vinegar, vanilla extract, lemon extract, and water. Add eggs, one at a time, beating well after each addition. Add melted butter, whisking to blend well. Pour egg mixture over sifted dry ingredients. Use the whisk to blend ingredients into a smooth batter. Immediately spoon batter into two greased and floured 9-inch pans. Bake for 35 to 40 minutes. Place the pan on wire rack to cool for five to ten minutes. Makes 14 servings.

- Cook's note: after melting, leave soy butter inside closed microwave to keep it liquid.

HEAVENLY CHOCOLATE FROSTING

2/3 cups Dutch-processed cocoa
1 cup natural sugar
1/2 cup of soy butter or unsalted organic butter
1/2 cup warm soymilk
2 teaspoons vanilla extract
1 teaspoon lemon extract

Mix cocoa and sugar; stir in melted butter. Add milk, lemon and vanilla extract. Using an electric mixer on medium speed, blend until smooth.
Nutritional information per iced cake serving: 386 cal.; total 14.79g fat; 9.77g protein 53.85g carb.; 274.19mg sodium
Dietary Exchanges 3.2 bread; 0 fruit/vegetable; .6 protein; 2.4 fat

CHOCOLATE SUPREME NON-DAIRY CREAM CHEESE FROSTING

16-ounces non-dairy cream cheese substitute
or Neufchatel cheese
1 tablespoon soy butter, or unsalted organic butter
1/2 cup Dutch-processed cocoa
3/4 cup natural sugar
2 teaspoons vanilla extract

Using an electric mixer on medium speed, blend cheese, butter and cocoa. Add vanilla extract, and continue mixing until sugar dissolves. Frost each layer with cream cheese.

Nutritional information per serving: 130.66 cal.; 9.59g total fat; 1.63g protein 9.31g carb.; 233.56 mg sodium

Dietary Exchanges .4 bread; 0 fruit/vegetable; .5 protein; 1.4 fat

HEAVENLY CHOCOLATE CAKE GOES EGGLESS

1 1/2 cups unbleached, all-purpose white flour
1 cup oat flour
1/2 cup Dutch-processed cocoa
1 1/2 cups natural sugar
1 teaspoon baking powder
2 teaspoons baking soda
2 tablespoons apple cider vinegar
2 teaspoons vanilla extract
1 teaspoon lemon extract
1 cup cold water
1 cup soymilk
1 cup soy butter, melted in microwave
for approximately 30 seconds, see note

Preheat oven to 350 degrees. Flour needs to be sifted twice. Sift unbleached flour and oat flour together the first time. For the second sifting, combine flour, cocoa, sugar, baking powder, and baking soda; set aside. Whisk together vinegar, vanilla extract, lemon extract, water and soy milk. Add melted butter, whisking to blend well. Pour vinegar/butter mixture over sifted dry ingredients. Use the whisk to blend ingredients into a smooth batter. Immediately spoon batter into two greased and floured 9-inch pans. Bake for 35 to 40 minutes. Cool pans on wire rack before frosting. Makes 14 servings.

• Cook's note: after melting, leave soy butter inside closed microwave to keep it liquid. Makes 14 servings.

Nutritional information per serving: 130.66 cal.; 9.59g total fat; 1.63g protein 9.31g carb.; 233.56 mg sodium

Dietary Exchanges .4 bread; 0 fruit/vegetable; .5 protein; 1.4 fat

SIMPLY SWEET BREAD

(1-stick) soy margarine or soy butter, softened
3/4 cup natural sugar
2 eggs
2 teaspoons vanilla extract
1 1/2 cup self-rising flour
1/3 cup soymilk

Preheat oven to 350 degrees. Grease and flour one 9-inch cake pan. Use a whisk to blend soy margarine and sugar. With a mixer set on medium speed, blend in eggs into margarine mixture, adding one at a time, blending well. Add vanilla extract and beat well. Add flour and milk to batter, alternatively, beginning and ending with flour.

Pour into prepared pan and bake for 30 minutes or until a wooden toothpick inserted near center of layer comes out clean. Remove from oven and place on a wire rack to cool. Makes 12 servings.

Nutritional information per serving: 164.59 cal.; 4.39g total fat; 4.29g protein 26.92g carb.; 232.01mg sodium

Dietary Exchanges 1.7 bread; 0 fruit/vegetable; .3 protein; .6 fat

OLD-FASHIONED BUTTERMILK POUND CAKE

1/2 cup soy butter or soy margarine, softened
1/2 cup soy butter, chilled in freezer for 45 minutes
1 1/4 cups natural sugar
1/2 cup unsweetened applesauce
5 organic eggs
2 teaspoons white vinegar
1 cup soymilk
1/8 teaspoon baking soda
3 cups all-purpose unbleached white flour
1/8 teaspoon sea salt
2 teaspoons vanilla extract
1 teaspoon almond extract

Preheat oven to 350 degrees. With an electric mixture on low speed, cream butter and shortening; gradually add sugar, beating well on medium speed. Add applesauce and eggs slowly, beating well after each egg addition. In a separate bowl, combine vinegar and soy milk. Dissolve baking soda in mixture; set aside.

Sift flour and salt together. Add to creamed mixture, alternating with soymilk mixture, beginning and ending with flour.

Stir in vanilla and almond extract. Pour batter into a greased and floured 10-inch tube pan. Bake for 40 to 50 minutes or until an inserted wooden pick comes out clean. Cool in pan 10 to 15 minutes before removing from pan to cool completely on wire rack. Makes 12 servings.

Nutritional information per serving: 357.11 cal.; 14.25g total fat; 7.95g protein 48.80g carb.; 173.04mg sodium

Dietary Exchanges 2.7 bread; 0 fruit/vegetable; .5 protein; 2.4 fat

CARROT CAKE

2 1/2 cups unbleached All-purpose organic white flour
2 teaspoons baking powder
2 teaspoons of cinnamon
1 teaspoon salt, optional
4 organic eggs
1 1/2 cups natural sugar
2 teaspoons vanilla extract
3 cups grated carrots
1/2 cup crushed walnuts
1/2 cup water
3/4 cup canola oil

Preheat oven to 350 degrees. Grease and flour two 9-inch cake pans; set aside. Sift together flour, baking powder, baking soda, cinnamon, sugar, and salt; set aside.

Use a whisk to beat eggs until frothy. Blend in vanilla extract and water. Slowly pour in oil, and whisk until mixture is well combined. Pour carrots and crushed nuts on top of sifted flour mixture; do not stir. Spoon egg mixture over flour and carrots. Use the whisk to blend ingredients into a smooth batter. Immediately spoon batter into greased and floured 9-inch cake pans. Bake for 35 to 40 minutes or until a wooden tester inserted into the center of each layer comes out clean. After removing from oven, place pans on wire rack. Cool completely before removing to frost. Makes 14 servings.

Nutritional information per serving: 498.14 cal.; total 26.57 g. fat; 10.18 g. protein 56.55 g. carb.; 445 mg. sodium; Dietary Exchanges 3.1 bread; .60 fruit/vegetable; 1 protein; 4.7 fat

VANILLA CREAM CHEESE FROSTING

16-ounces non-dairy cream cheese substitute or Neufchatel cheese
1 tablespoon soy butter or unsalted organic butter
3/4 cup natural sugar
2 teaspoons vanilla extract
1 cup grated carrots
1/2 cup crushed walnuts

Blend cheese and butter using an electric mixer on low speed. Add sugar and vanilla extract and continue mixing until sugar dissolves. Frost each layer with cream cheese. Sprinkle nuts and carrots on top of cream cheese for garnish.

Nutritional information per serving: 119.18 cal.; 7.94g total fat; 3.62g protein 8.52g carb.; 134.10 mg sodium Dietary Exchanges .4 bread; 0 fruit/vegetable; .5 protein; 1.4 fat

RED VELVET CAKE

4 tablespoons Dutch-processed cocoa
2 (1-ounce) bottles natural red food coloring
2 cups all-purpose unbleached white flour
1/2 cup wheat pastry flour or oat flour
or 2 1/2 cups all purpose unbleached white flour
1/4 teaspoon salt
1 tablespoon white vinegar
1 teaspoon baking soda
1 cup soy milk
1/2 cup vegetable oil
1 1/2 cups natural sugar
2 organic eggs
1 tablespoon unsweetened applesauce
1 teaspoon vanilla extract
1 teaspoon almond extract

Preheat oven to 350 degrees. In a small bowl, combine cocoa and natural food coloring; set aside. Sift together flours and salt; set aside. In a separate bowl, stir vinegar and baking soda into soymilk; set aside.

Using a mixer set on medium speed, cream oil, sugar and eggs until batter becomes fluffy. Add cocoa paste to this batter. Mix in sifted flour, alternating dry ingredients with soymilk mixture. Add applesauce, vanilla extract, and almond extract. Pour batter into three greased and floured 9-inch cake pans or two pans lined with parchment paper. Bake in oven for 30 to 40 minutes or until a wooden toothpick inserted near center of each layer comes out clean. Makes 14 servings.

Nutritional information per serving: 458.77 cal.; 21.84g total fat; 7.85g protein 58.79g carb.; 208.83mg sodium

Dietary Exchanges 3.5 bread; 0 fruit/vegetable; .4 protein; 3.9 fat

CREAM CHEESE FROSTING

16 ounces non-dairy cream cheese substitute or
16-ounces Neufchatel cheese
1/2 cup natural sugar
1 tablespoon soy margarine
2 teaspoons vanilla extract

Using a mixture on medium speed, combine all ingredients until smooth and creamy. Makes 14 servings.

Nutritional information per serving: 119 cal.; 7.94g total fat; 3.62g protein; 8.52g carb.; 134.10mg. sodium

Dietary Exchanges .4 bread; 0 fruit/vegetable; .5 protein; 1.4 fat

PINEAPPLE COCONUT CAKE

2 1/2 cups unbleached all-purpose white flour
2 teaspoons baking powder
3/4 teaspoon salt, optional
3/4 cup vegetable shortening
1 cup natural sugar
4 organic eggs
1 cup soymilk
3/4 cup of unsweetened crushed pineapples, drained
2 teaspoons coconut extract
1 teaspoon almond extract

Preheat oven to 350 degrees. In medium bowl, sift flour, baking powder and salt; set aside. Cream shortening and sugar; beat well. Add eggs, one at a time, beating after each addition. With a mixer on medium speed, blend in flour mixture alternately with soymilk, ending with the flour mixture. Stir in pineapples, coconut extract and almond extract. Pour batter into two greased and floured 9-inch cake pans or two pans lined with parchment paper. Bake for 25 to 30 minutes or until a wooden pick is inserted in the center of each layer and comes out clean.

Remove pans from oven; run a dull dinner knife around sides to prevent sticking. Let cool on wire racks for 15 minutes. Remove layers from pan to completely cool before frosting. Makes 12 servings.

Nutritional information per serving: 406.97cal.; 21.34g total fat; 7.49g protein 46.78g carb.; 191.25mg sodium

Dietary Exchanges 2.3 bread; 0 fruit/vegetable; .6 protein; 3.9 fat

PINEAPPLE COCONUT FROSTING

8-ounces Neufchatel cheese
1 tablespoon soy butter
1/2 cup natural sugar
1/2 cup unsweetened fresh or frozen coconut flakes
1/2 cup unsweetened crushed pineapple, drained

With a mixer on low speed, blend cheese and butter; add sugar and coconut. Continue beating until light and fluffy. Mix in pineapple. Frost each layer with creamy frosting. Makes 12 servings.

Nutritional information per serving: 163.76 cal.; 12.09g total fat; 3.48g protein 11.70g carb.; 114.55mg sodium

Dietary Exchanges .5 bread; 0 fruit/vegetable; .5 protein; 2.2 fat

CINNAMON PECAN KOFFEE CAKE TOPPING:

1/3 cup natural sugar
2 teaspoons ground cinnamon
1/2 cup chopped pecans

Preheat oven to 350 degrees. To make topping: combine sugar, cinnamon and chopped pecans in a small bowl; set aside. To make cake: Sift flours, baking powder, baking soda, and salt; set aside. With an electric mixer on medium speed, blend soy butter with 3/4 cup of sugar until light and fluffy. Beat in applesauce. Add eggs one at a time and beat after each addition. Add almond extract. Spoon flour mixture into batter alternating with sour cream, beginning and ending with flour mixture. Spoon half of the batter into a greased 10-inch tube pan. Use a dinner knife to lightly swirl topping through batter. Pour in remaining batter. Bake at 350 degrees for 50 minutes or until done. Makes 14 servings.

Nutritional information per serving: 275.55 cal.; 11g total fat; 6.38g protein; 38.66g carb.; 325mg sodium

Dietary Exchanges 2.2 bread; 0 fruit/vegetable; .5 protein; 2 fat

CAKE

1 1/2 cup all-purpose unbleached white flour
1/2 cup whole wheat pastry flour
1 teaspoon baking powder
1 teaspoon baking soda
1/2 teaspoon salt
1/2 cup soy butter or organic unsalted butter, softened
3/4 cup natural sugar
2 tablespoons of unsweetened applesauce
Egg substitute equal to 2 eggs or 2 organic eggs
8-ounces non-dairy sour cream substitute or organic sour cream
1 teaspoon almond extract

LEMON POPPY SEED CAKE

3/4 cup soy butter, melted
8-ounces non-dairy cream cheese substitute
6 organic eggs
3 cups all-purpose unbleached
self-rising white flour, sifted
1 teaspoon baking powder
1/4 teaspoon salt
1 1/2 cup natural sugar
1/8 cup poppy seeds
2 teaspoons lemon extract

Allow cream cheese and eggs to stand at room temperature for 30 minutes. Meanwhile, melt soy butter. Grease and lightly flour a 10-inch tube pan; set aside. Sift together flour, baking powder and salt; set aside.

With a mixer on low to medium speed, beat soy butter and cheese until creamy, approximately 30 seconds. Gradually add sugar, 2 tablespoons at a time, beating after each addition. Continue beating for about five minutes or until batter becomes very light and fluffy. Mix in poppy seeds and lemon extract.

With the mixer on low speed, add eggs, one at a time, beating after each addition; scrape the bowl frequently. Keeping the mixer on low speed, slowly add flour mixture, beating just to combine.

Pour batter into prepared pan. Bake in a 325 degree oven about 50 minutes or until a wooden toothpick inserted near center of each layer comes out clean. Cool in pan on wire rack 15 minutes. Remove cake from pan and cool thoroughly on wire rack. Makes 12 servings.

Nutritional information per serving: 367.73 cal.; 13.24g total fat; 12.06g protein 49.69g carb.; 263.34mg sodium
Dietary Exchanges 2.8 bread; 0 fruit/vegetable; 1 protein; 1.8 fat

SWEET MOLASSES BREAD

1 1/2 cups of unbleached all-purpose white flour
1/2 cup of oat flour
1 teaspoon cinnamon
1 teaspoon baking powder
1 teaspoon baking soda
1/2 cup vegetable shortening
3/4 cup natural sugar
2 organic eggs
1/3 cup raw molasses
1/2 cup water
1 teaspoon vanilla extract

Preheat oven to 350 degrees. Grease and flour a 6-by-11-inch loaf pan; set aside. Sift together flour, cinnamon, baking powder and baking soda; set aside. With a mixer on medium speed, blend shortening and sugar until light and creamy. Add eggs, one at a time, beating after each addition. Blend in molasses. Add flour mixture, alternating with water. Spoon batter into loaf pan. Bake for 40 to 45 minutes. Makes 12 servings.

Nutritional information per serving: 250.79 cal.; 5.51g total fat; 6.39g protein 44.70g carb.; 244.8mg sodium
Dietary Exchanges 2.6 bread; 0 fruit/vegetable; .4 protein; .7 fat

HUMMING BIRD CAKE

3 cups all-purpose unbleached white flour or 2
1/2 cups unbleached all-purpose flour sifted with
1/2 cup wheat or oat flour
1 teaspoon ground cinnamon
1 teaspoon ground nutmeg
1 teaspoon baking soda
1/2 teaspoon salt
3/4 cup soy butter or 3/4 cup vegetable oil
1 cup natural sugar
3 organic eggs
2 cups ripe bananas, mashed
1 (8-ounce) can unsweetened crushed pineapple
2 teaspoons vanilla extract
3/4 cup chopped pecans

Preheat oven to 350 degrees. Sift together flour, cinnamon, nutmeg, baking soda, and salt; set aside. Using an electric mixer on medium speed, cream soy butter, and sugar, mixing well. Add eggs one at a time, beating well after each addition. Blend in mashed bananas, pineapple, pecans and vanilla extract.

Pour batter into three greased and floured 9-inch cake pans, or three pans lined with parchment paper. Bake for 30 minutes, or until a wooden toothpick inserted near center of each layer comes out clean. Remove cake from pan and cool thoroughly on wire rack. Makes 12 servings.

Nutritional information per serving: 357.11 cal.; 14.25g total fat; 7.95g protein 48.80g carb.; 173.04mg sodium
Dietary Exchanges 2.7 bread; 0 fruit/vegetable; .5 protein; 2.4 fat

CREAM CHEESE FROSTING

1 (8-ounce package) Neufchatel cheese
1/4 cup vegetable oil
3/4 cup natural sugar
1 teaspoon vanilla

With an electric mixer on medium speed, blend all ingredients until smooth and creamy. Makes 12 servings.
Nutritional information per serving: 139cal.; 4.02g total fat; 9.26g protein 9.9g carb.; 156.45mg sodium
Dietary Exchanges .5 bread; 0 fruit/vegetable; .6 protein; 1.6 fat

ESSENCE OF BLACK CAKE

1 pound pitted prunes or dried grapes
1 pound seedless raisins
1 1/2 pounds seedless dates
1/2 pound citron
1 1/2 cup brandy
1 1/2 cup dark rum
1 1/2 cup port wine
2/3 cup of Amaretto
1/2 cup chopped walnuts
1/8 teaspoon ground allspice
1/8 teaspoon ground nutmeg
1 1/2 cup soy margarine or soy butter
2 cups natural sugar
10 organic eggs, beaten
1 teaspoon vanilla extract
3 cups soy flour or unbleached all-purpose white flour
3 tablespoons burnt sugar, see note
2 teaspoons baking powder

Place all fruit (except cherries) and nuts in food processor container jar. Process and place chopped fruit into a large plastic container. Pour brandy, rum liqueur, and one cup of port wine over processed fruit and nuts. Seal mixture tightly and allow to set at room temperature for 12 to 24 hours.

When ready to prepare cake, grease and flour two Bundt pans; set aside. Sift soy flour and baking powder; set aside. With a mixer on medium speed, cream soy margarine and sugar. Add beaten eggs, vanilla extract, allspice and nutmeg. Blend in flour mixture. Stir in burnt sugar. Use a wooden spoon to stir in fruit and nut mixture until well-blended. Mixture should be the consistency of cake batter. If batter is too thick, add additional 1/3 to 1/2 cup wine. Pour batter into two Bundt pans. Bake at 350 degrees for 60-75 minutes or until cake begins to pull away from the side of the pan. Use remaining 1/2 cup of wine to pour on top of cakes as soon as they come out of the oven. Cool on wire racks before removing cakes from pans. Makes two cakes, 18 servings each.

Note: Purchase burnt sugar

- Cook's Health Note: The Essence of Black Cake is not recommended for anyone on a therapeutic diet especially for weight, diabetes, blood pressure, or heart disease.

Nutritional information per serving: 406 cal.; 10.58g total fat; 4.6g protein; 61.33g carb.;203mg sodium

Dietary Exchanges 1.8 bread; 1.3 fruit/ 2.0 vegetable; .5 protein; 3.5 fat

STRAWBERRY SHORT CAKE

3 cups of fresh or frozen strawberries
1/4 cup, plus 1/3 cup natural sugar
1/2 solid vegetable shortening
2 cups all-purpose unbleached white flour
2 teaspoons baking powder
1/4 teaspoon salt (optional)
1/2 cup soymilk
1 teaspoon vanilla extract
2 organic eggs
1 (7-ounce) can non-dairy whipped cream substitute

Preheat oven to 450 degrees. Grease and flour two 9-inch cake pans; set aside. Combine whole strawberries and 1/4 cup of sugar in a saucepan. Cook for 10 minutes over low heat; set aside.

Sift together flour, baking soda, and salt. Cut in shortening using two dull knives to achieve a mixture that resembles a coarse meal. Add egg yolk substitute, sugar, milk, and vanilla extract to flour mixture.

Stir batter with a fork to form a sticky, wet dough. Use a spoon to spread dough evenly between two 9-inch cake pans. Bake at 450 degrees for 12 minutes or until layers are done. Remove from pans and let cool completely on wire racks. Dough will not rise in the traditional pattern of a cake.

Use a knife to cut each layer in half. Prepare short cakes by layering an even amount of strawberries and non-dairy whipping topping on each layer. Makes 12 servings.

Nutritional information per serving: 257.43 cal.; 13.28g total fat; 3.73g protein 30.42g carb.; 94.60mg sodium

Dietary Exchanges 1.3 bread; 0 fruit/vegetable; .3 protein; 3.1 fat

YELLOW CAKE

2 1/4 cups unbleached all-purpose white flour
2 teaspoons baking powder
3/4 teaspoon salt, optional
3/4 cup vegetable shortening
1 cup natural sugar
4 organic eggs
1 cup soymilk
2 teaspoons vanilla extract
1 teaspoon almond extract

Preheat oven to 350 degrees. Sift flour, baking powder and salt; set aside. Cream shortening and sugar; beat well. Add eggs, one at a time, beating after each addition. Add flour mixture alternating with milk. Mix well. Stir in vanilla extract. Pour batter into 2 greased and floured 9-inch cake pans or 2 pans lined with parchment paper. Bake for 25 to 30 minutes. Remove from oven; cool on wire rack before frosting. Makes 12 servings.

Nutritional information per serving: 263 cal.; 7.29g total fat; 8.15g protein 40.42g carb.; 171.22mg sodium.

Dietary Exchanges 2.4 bread; 0 fruit/vegetable; .6 protein; 1 fat

WHITE CAKE

2 1/4 cups unbleached self rising white flour
3/4 teaspoon salt
3/4 cup vegetable shortening
1 cup natural sugar
1 cup soymilk
2 teaspoons clear vanilla extract
6 organic egg whites

Preheat oven to 350 degrees. Flour needs to be sifted twice. Sift it alone the first time. For the second sifting, combine flour, baking powder and salt; set aside. With a mixer on medium speed, cream vegetable shortening and sugar. Add egg whites, one at a time, beating well after each addition. Add flour mixture alternately with soymilk; mix well. Stir in vanilla and almond extract. Spoon batter into two greased and floured 9-inch cake pans or two greased pans lined with parchment paper. Bake for 25 to 30 minutes. Remove from oven and let cool on wire rack before frosting. Makes 12 servings.

Nutritional information per serving: 331.81 cal.; 16.12g total fat; 5.26g protein 41.57g carb.; 387.79mg sodium.

Dietary Exchanges 2.4 bread; 0 fruit/vegetable; .3 protein; 3.1 fat

CAKE OF MANY FLAVORS

2 1/4 cups unbleached all-purpose white flour
2 teaspoons baking powder
1 teaspoon of baking soda
3/4 teaspoon salt, optional
3/4 cup vegetable shortening or soy butter
1 1/4 cup natural sugar
4 eggs, beaten
1 teaspoon vanilla extract
1 teaspoon coconut extract
1 teaspoon almond extract
1 teaspoon butter flavor
1 cup soymilk

Preheat oven to 350 degrees. Sift together flour, baking powder, baking soda and salt; set aside. With a mixer on medium speed, cream shortening and sugar; beat well. Mix in eggs, one at a time, beating after each addition. Add vanilla extract, almond extract, coconut extract, and butter flavor to flour mixture, alternating with milk, and ending with flour. Pour batter into two greased and floured 9-inch cake pans or two greased pans lined with parchment paper. Bake 25 to 30 minutes or until an inserted wooden pick comes out clean from each layer. Remove from oven and let cool on wire rack. Makes 10 servings.

Nutritional information per serving: 379.4 cal.; 18.12g total; 6.12g protein; 47.55g carb.; 252.45mg. sodium

Dietary Exchanges 2.8 bread; 0 fruit/vegetable; .4 protein; 3.3 fat

Cheesecakes &

I first learned about cheesecake during high school. I learned about many things during the 70's but it was my first introduction to the cheesecake. I was the first to bake cheesecake in my family. Where I lived people were not apt to try something that they were unsure about. The first cheesecake I ever tasted was by Jello. I knew I was a great cook, but I swear this cheesecake made me want to give up some of my favorites. I must have made cheesecakes for a month straight. They were great! All of my friends would come over after school so we could talk about our homework, what teachers worked our last nerve, our love life and our new outfits. I

fruit toppings

would serve desserts and they would say how I was going to keep my man because I was such a good cook.

I had not eaten cheesecake in over four years when I began creating my luscious creamy cheesecake with dairy alternatives. I do create other cheesecakes, but because there are so many allergies in my family, I create dessert recipes that will support healthy living.

I was working with cheesecake recipes the week of September 11, 2001, and I, like most of the country, felt very unsettled and uncertain. I had worked on several of my refrigerated cheesecakes, but everything I touched

seemed to come out wrong. Watching the tragic events caused me to feel very stressed , so I decided to turn off the television. It would be on that afternoon of September 11, 2001, that I would create a specially baked Cheesecake I entitled "New York On My Mind Cheesecake." Food has always been a source of comfort to me and I feel it has helped bring people and families together. My cheesecake was not only delicious but it was my way of giving something back. In an effort to make the faculty and staff feel better as they coped with these tragic events I made some cheesecake for them.

21

LUSCIOUS CREAMY CHEESECAKE

2 envelopes unflavored Emes Kosher- Jel or 2
envelopes unflavored gelatin
3/4 cup natural sugar
3/4 cup boiling water
4 (8-ounce) packages Neufchatel cheese
or 32-ounces non-dairy
cream cheese substitute, soften
1 teaspoon vanilla extract
2 teaspoons lemon extract
1 (9-inch) graham cracker crust, prepared with
whole wheat graham crackers

Mix Emes Kosher-Jel (or gelatin) and sugar in small bowl. Add boiling water. Stir until powder dissolves; set aside. Using an electric mixer on low speed, beat cheese until smooth; add vanilla and lemon extracts. Add dissolved gelatin to cheese, one third at a time, beating well after each addition. Spoon mixture over prepared crust. Garnish as desired.

Refrigerate two hours or freeze 30 minutes before serving. Makes 10 servings.

Nutritional information per serving: 298.65cal.; 19.42 total g. fat; 8.38g. protein 23.82g. carb.; 358.52 mg. sodium
Dietary Exchanges 1.3 bread;
1 fruit/vegetable; 1 protein; 3.3 fat

HONEY GRAHAM PIECRUST

1 1/2 cups crushed graham crackers
1 tablespoon natural sugar
1/2 cup soy margarine or organic unsalted butter

Combine all ingredients until well mixed. Firmly press mixture evenly over bottom and sides of a 9-inch pie plate. Bake at 325 degrees for 10 minutes. Makes six or eight servings.

Nutritional information per six serving: 199.32 cal.; 7.20g total fat; 4.61g protein; 29.29g carb.; 236.35 mg. sodium
Nutritional information per eight servings:149.49 cal.; 6.40g total fat; 3.46g protein; 21.96g carb.; 236.35 mg. sodium
Dietary Exchanges 1.9 bread; 0 fruit/vegetable; 0 protein; .8 fat

LUSCIOUS CREAMY LEMON CHEESECAKE

2 envelopes unflavored Emes Kosher- Jel or 2 envelopes unflavored gelatin
3/4 cup natural sugar
3/4 cup boiling water
4 (8-ounce) packages Neufchatel cheese or 32-ounces non-dairy cream cheese substitute, soften
1 teaspoon vanilla extract
2 teaspoons lemon extract
1 teaspoon lemon zest
1 (10-inch) graham cracker crust, prepared with whole wheat graham crackers

Mix Emes Kosher-Jel (or gelatin) and sugar in small bowl. Add boiling water. Stir until powder dissolves; set aside. Using an electric mixer on low speed, beat cheese until smooth; add vanilla extract, lemon extract, and lemon zest. Add dissolved gelatin to cheese, one third at a time, beating well after each addition. Spoon mixture over prepared crust. Garnish as desired.

Refrigerate for two hours or freeze for 30 minutes before serving. Makes 10 servings.

Nutritional information per serving: 300.34 cal.;16.5g total fat; 6.9g protein; 32.08g carb.; 320.94mg. sodium

Dietary Exchanges 1.9 bread; 1 fruit/vegetable; .7 protein; 2.8 fat

LUSCIOUS CHERRY CHEESECAKE

2 envelopes unflavored Emes Kosher- Jel or 2 envelopes unflavored gelatin
3/4 cup natural sugar
3/4 cup boiling water
2 (8-ounce) package Neufchatel cheese or 8-ounces non-dairy cream cheese substitute, soften
2 teaspoons vanilla extract
1/2 cup fresh or frozen cherries or use 1/2 cup Maraschino cherries, finely chopped
1 (9-inch) graham-cracker crust, prepared with whole wheat graham crackers
Red cherries for garnish, optional

Mix Emes Kosher-Jel (or gelatin) and sugar in small bowl. Add boiling water and stir until powder dissolves; set aside. Using an electric mixer on low speed, beat cheese until smooth; add vanilla extract. Add dissolved gelatin to cheese, one third at a time, beating well after each addition. Add 1/2 cup of chopped cherries. Spoon mixture over prepared crust. Garnish with cherries, if desired. Refrigerate for two hours or freeze for 30 minutes before serving. Makes 10 servings.

Nutritional information per serving: 306.46 cal.; 16.67 total g. fat; .7g. protein 33.21g. carb.; 321 mg. sodium

Dietary Exchanges 1.9 bread; 1 fruit/vegetable; 1 protein; 2.8 fat

DREAMY CHOCOLATE CHEESECAKE

2 envelopes unflavored Emes Kosher- Jel
or 2 envelopes unflavored gelatin
3/4 cup natural sugar
3/4 cup boiling water
2 (8-ounce) package Neufchatel cheese,
softened or 16-ounces non-dairy cream cheese substitute
2 teaspoons lemon extract
1/2 cup of unprocessed Dutch chocolate or carob
1 (9-inch) graham-cracker crust,
prepared with whole wheat graham crackers

Mix Emes Kosher-Jel (or gelatin) and sugar in small bowl. Add boiling water. Stir until powder dissolves; set aside. Using an electric mixer on low speed, beat cheese until smooth; add lemon extract. Add gelatin mixture to cheese, one third at a time, beating well after each addition. Add chocolate, beating slowly to blend well. Spoon mixture over prepared crust. Garnish as desired. Refrigerate two hours or freeze 30 minutes before serving. Makes 10 servings.

Nutritional information per serving: 319.08 cal.; 16.98g total fat; 7.79g. protein 34.51g. carb.; 323.11 mg. sodium
Dietary Exchanges 2 bread; 1 fruit/vegetable; .7 protein; 2.8 fat

PINEAPPLE UPSIDE DOWN CHEESECAKE

2 envelopes unflavored Emes Kosher-Jel
or 2 envelopes unflavored gelatin
3/4 cup, plus 1 tablespoon natural sugar
3/4 cup boiling water
2 (8-ounce) packages Neufchatel cheese
or 16-ounces non-dairy cream cheese substitute, soften
2 teaspoons pineapple extract
1 (9-inch) graham cracker crust,
prepared with whole wheat graham crackers
1 (8-ounce) can unsweetened pineapple slices, drained

Mix Emes Kosher-Jel (or gelatin) and sugar in small bowl. Add boiling water. Stir until powder dissolves; set aside. Using an electric mixer on low speed, beat cheese until smooth; add pineapple extract. Add dissolved gelatin to cheese, one third at a time, beating after each addition. Arrange pineapple slices over prepared crust. Sprinkle with one tablespoon of sugar. Spoon over prepared crust. Garnish, if desired.

Refrigerate two hours or freeze 30 minutes before serving. Makes 10 servings.

Nutritional information per serving: 314.58 cal.; 16.59g total fat; 7.06g protein 35.20g carb.; 321.24 mg. sodium
Dietary Exchanges 1.9 bread; 1 fruit/vegetable; .7 protein; 2.8 fat

LACEY CINNAMON CHEESECAKE

**2 envelopes unflavored Emes Kosher- Jel or
2 envelopes unflavored gelatin
3/4 cup natural sugar
3/4 cup boiling water
2 (8-ounce) package Neufchatel cheese,
softened or 16-ounces non-dairy cream
cheese substitute
1 teaspoon vanilla extract
2 teaspoons ground cinnamon
1 teaspoon ground nutmeg
1 (9-inch) graham-cracker crust, prepared
with whole wheat graham crackers
Melted carob or melted semi-sweet
chocolate, optional for garnish**

Mix Emes Kosher-Jel (or gelatin) and sugar in small bowl. Add boiling water. Stir until powder dissolves; set aside. Using an electric mixer on low speed, beat cheese until smooth; add vanilla extract, cinnamon and nutmeg. Add dissolved gelatin to cheese, one third at a time, beating well after each addition. Spoon mixture over prepared crust. Garnish, if desired.

Refrigerate two hours or freeze for 30 minutes before serving. Makes 10 servings.

Nutritional information per serving: 302.4cal.; 16.67g total fat; 7g protein 32.43g carb.; 321.08 mg. sodium
Dietary Exchanges 1.9 bread;
1 fruit/vegetable; .6 protein; 2.8 fat

SWEETER THAN SWEET POTATO CHEESECAKE

1 1/2 envelopes unflavored Emes Kosher-Jel
or 1 1/2 envelopes unflavored gelatin
3/4 cup natural sugar
3/4 cup boiling water
2 (8-ounce) packages Neufchatel cheese
or 16-ounces non-dairy cream cheese substitute, soften
2 teaspoons vanilla extract
1 large sweet potato, baked, peeled
1 teaspoon ground cinnamon
1/2 teaspoon ground nutmeg
1 (9-inch) graham cracker crust,
prepared with whole wheat graham crackers
Optional Cinnamon/Pecan garnish:
1/2 cup crushed pecans
1 teaspoon cinnamon
1 teaspoon natural sugar

Mash baked sweet potato with cinnamon and nutmeg; set aside. Mix Emes Kosher-Jel (or gelatin) and sugar in small bowl. Add boiling water. Stir until powder dissolves; set aside.

Using an electric mixer on low speed, beat cheese until smooth; add vanilla extract. Add dissolved mixture to cheese, one third at a time, beating well after each addition. In a separate bowl, combine one third of the cheese mixture with the seasoned mashed sweet potato; reserve.

Spoon half of plain cheese mixture into prepared crust. Chill in freezer for 10 minutes. Remove and spoon reserved sweet potato and cheese blend over chilled mixture.

To prepare optional Cinnamon/Pecan garnish: place pecans, cinnamon and sugar in a saucepan and heat until sugar melts. Drizzle over cheesecake.

Refrigerate two hours or freeze 30 minutes before serving. Makes 10 servings.

Nutritional information per serving: 323.96 cal.; 16.63g total fat; 6.99g protein 37.45g carb.; 353.22mg. sodium
Dietary Exchanges 2.1 bread; 1 fruit/vegetable; .7 protein; 2.8 fat

BERRY BLUEBERRY CHEESECAKE

2 envelopes unflavored Emes Kosher- Jel
or 2 envelopes unflavored gelatin
3/4 cup natural sugar
3/4 cup boiling water
2 (8-ounce) packages Neufchatel cheese, softened
1 teaspoon vanilla extract
1/2 cup fresh or frozen blueberries, chopped
1 cup fresh or frozen blueberries, thinly sliced
1/2 cup crushed whole wheat graham crackers
1 (9-inch) graham cracker crust,
prepared with whole wheat graham crackers

Mix Emes Kosher-Jel (or gelatin) and sugar in small bowl. Add boiling water. Stir until powder dissolves; set aside. Using an electric mixer on low speed, beat cheese until smooth; add vanilla extract. Add dissolved gelatin to cheese, one third at a time, beating well after each addition. Add 1/2 cup finely chopped blueberries. Spoon over prepared crust.

Garnish with sliced blueberries and 1/2 cup of crushed whole wheat grahams.

Refrigerate for two hours or freeze 30 minutes before serving. Makes 10 servings.

Nutritional information per serving: 312.06 cal.;16.67 total g. fat; 7.09g. protein 34.47g. carb.; 320 mg. sodium
Dietary Exchanges 1.9 bread; 1 fruit/vegetable; .7 protein; 2.8 fat

TUTTI FRUITTI CHEESECAKE

1/2 cup red maraschino cherries
1/2 cup green maraschino cherries
2 envelopes unflavored Emes Kosher- Jel
or 2 envelopes unflavored gelatin
3/4 cup natural sugar
3/4 cup boiling water
2 (8-ounce) packages Neufchatel cheese
or 16-ounces non-dairy cream cheese substitute, soften
1 teaspoon vanilla extract
2 teaspoons almond extract
1 (9-inch) graham cracker crust,
prepared with whole wheat graham

Mix red and green cherries and cover with cold water. Combine Emes Kosher-Jel (or gelatin) and sugar in a small bowl. Add boiling water and stir until powder dissolves; set aside. Using an electric mixer on low speed, beat cheese until smooth. Add vanilla and almond extract to cheese. Add dissolved gelatin to cheese, one third at a time, beating well after each addition. Drain cherries and add 1/2 cup of mixed green and red cherries to cheese mixture; mix well. Pour into prepared crust. Garnish with remaining cherries.

Refrigerate for two hours or freeze for 30 minutes before serving. Makes 10 servings.

Nutritional information per serving: 338.87 cal.; 16.63g total fat; 7g protein; 41.97g carb.; 321.09 mg. sodium

Dietary Exchanges 1.9 bread; .6 fruit/vegetable; 1 protein; 2.8 fat

BANANA PUDDING CHEESECAKE

2 medium ripe bananas
1 teaspoon ground cinnamon
1 1/2 envelopes unflavored Emes Kosher- Jel
or unflavored gelatin
3/4 cup natural sugar
2 (8-ounce) packages Neufchatel cheese
or 8-ounces non-dairy
cream cheese alternative, soften
3/4 cup boiling water
2 teaspoons lemon extract
1 (9-inch) prepared organic
vanilla wafer piecrust

Mash bananas with cinnamon and set aside. Mix Emes Kosher-Jel (or gelatin) and sugar in small bowl. Add boiling water. Stir until powder dissolves; set aside. Using an electric mixer on low speed, beat cheese until smooth; add lemon extract. Add dissolved gelatin to cheese, one third at a time, beating well after each addition. Add bananas and blend well. Spoon mixture over prepared crust. Garnish as desired. Refrigerate two hours or freeze 30 minutes before serving. Makes 10 servings.

• Note: See Vanilla Wafer Pie Crust

Nutritional information per serving: 381.24cal.; 17.57 total g. fat; 6.96 g. protein 32.28 g. carb.; 320.51 mg. sodium

Dietary Exchanges 1.9 bread; 1 fruit/vegetable; .7 protein; 2.8 fat

BLACKBERRY CHEESECAKE

2 envelopes unflavored Emes Kosher- Jel
or unflavored gelatin
3/4 cup natural sugar
3/4 cup boiling water
2 (8-ounce) packages Neufchatel cheese or 16-ounces
non-dairy cream cheese alternative, soften
1 teaspoon lemon extract
1/2 cup of blackberry jelly
1/2 cup of blackberry jam
1 teaspoon vanilla extract
1 (9-inch) graham cracker crust,
prepared with whole wheat graham crackers

Mix Emes Kosher-Jel (or gelatin) and sugar in a small bowl. Add boiling water. Stir until powder dissolves; set aside. Using an electric mixer on low speed, beat cheese until smooth; add lemon extract. Add dissolved gelatin to cheese, one third at a time, beating well after each addition. Add blackberry jelly and beat well. Stir in blackberry jam slowly. Spoon over prepared crust. Garnish as desired.

Refrigerate two hours or freeze 30 minutes before serving. Makes 10 servings.

Nutritional information per serving: 381.24 cal.; 16.57 total g. fat; 6.96g. protein 52.81g. carb.; 337 mg. sodium

Dietary Exchanges 3.5 bread; 1 fruit/vegetable; .7 protein; 2.8 fat

FRUITTI TOPPINGS FOR CHEESECAKE

3 cups fresh or frozen strawberry slices or chopped
blueberries, blackberries, pineapple chunks or peeled,
pitted and chopped peaches
1/2 to 1/3 cup water
3 tablespoons of cornstarch
1/2 cup natural sugar
2 teaspoons lemon juice

If using frozen berries, thaw. Mix fruit and remaining ingredients and bring to a boil. Reduce heat and cook until mixture thickens. Remove from heat. Cool before topping cheesecake.

Nutritional information per serving: 50.93 cal.; .05g total fat; .21g protein; 13.09g carb.; 1.43 mg. sodium

Dietary Exchanges .6 bread; .3 fruit/vegetable; 0 protein; 0 fat

"NEW YORK ON MY MIND" CHEESECAKE

1/2 cup soy butter, melted
4 (8-ounce) packages of Neufchatel cheese or
32 ounces non-dairy cream cheese substitute, at
room temperature
3/4 cup natural sugar
2 tablespoons cornstarch
1 teaspoon vanilla extract
2 teaspoons lemon extract
2 organic eggs
1/4 cup unflavored soymilk
1-10 inch whole wheat graham crust

Preheat oven to 375 degrees. Using a mixer on medium speed, beat cream cheese, sugar, and melted soy butter. Add cornstarch, vanilla extract, lemon extract and soymilk; beat well. Add eggs, one at a time, beating after each addition.

Add milk and continue mixing until smooth and creamy. Spoon mixture into prepared crust. Bake for 35 to 40 minutes in a 10-inch springform pan. Cool in pan for 40 minutes on wire rack. Cover pan with plastic wrap. Freeze for one hour or refrigerate for three hours. Makes 14 servings.

Nutritional information per serving: 381.81 cal.; 13.32g total fat; 11.49g protein; 33.91g carb.; 426.29 mg. sodium

Dietary Exchanges 2.1 bread; 0 fruit/vegetable; 1.3 protein; 3.5 fat

KINDERGARTEN CHANGED MY LIFE FOREVER. I BECAME A MEMBER OF THE "STEEL MARBLE CLUB" AND THERE WAS ONLY ONE WAY IN AND ONE WAY OUT.

When I was in kindergarten, I attended a two-room school house with several of my siblings. Although mom always prepared our lunch, we would buy a Big Jack Cookie and a carton of chocolate milk. I learned to shoot marbles at age five. The boys at my school would do almost anything if they could win what was called the steel marble. I liked winning, especially when I was competing against the boys. I was better than most of those guys, if I must say so myself. They tried to keep me out of the game because it was a marble club for boys at least that's what they thought. When the captain, Charlie Brown, fell in love with me all the rules of the game began to change. I became an official member of the Steele Marble Club. It wasn't long before they were calling me "Keeper of

Cookies

the Steel Marbles." My bag of steel marbles made me the envy of them all. I would trade most of my steel marbles back for their Big Jack Cookies. By lunch-time I would have at least a half dozen cookies for lunch. Life was great. At the age of five I was the only girl who could make boys cry just to get back an old marble.

The first cookie I remember was my mother's teacakes cookies. Baby, you have not had a cookie until you have had one of my mother's teacakes. When I asked my mother how she made the teacakes, she told me that her mother and grandmother would sample a cake by testing several small portions of cake batter in a pan which turned out to be cookies or teacakes for me.

Many of the cookies I baked, as a mother, were from store-bought cookie dough. Of course, I made sure I had a supply for each week. After I gave birth to my son, I stopped baking as much so that I would have more time to spend with him. However, my love for cookies remained strong whether I was baking or buying them. When I began to write "Naturally Yours Gourmet Desserts," it was important to me that I created cookie recipes that were tasty and healthy. I used ingredients with fiber and vitamins to support a healthy lifestyle. I think you will be very pleased with my cookie section. There are some excellent recipes and great selections for children. I hope that you have as much fun as I did preparing them.

OATMEAL RAISIN COOKIES

1 cup unbleached all-purpose white flour
1/2 cup pastry wheat flour or 1/2 cup oat flour
1 teaspoon baking soda
2 teaspoons ground cinnamon
1/2 teaspoon salt
3/4 cup vegetable oil or soy margarine
3/4 cup natural sugar
2 organic eggs or egg substitutes that equal 2 eggs
2 tablespoons applesauce
1 teaspoon vanilla extract
3/4 cup raisins
2 cups old-fashioned uncooked oatmeal
3/4 cup finely chopped pecans, optional

Preheat oven to 350 degrees. Combine flours, baking soda, cinnamon, and salt; set aside. In a mixer bowl, cream vegetable oil and sugar. Add eggs, vanilla, and applesauce, mix well. Add flour mixture to creamed mixture and beat just until blended. Stir in oats, raisins, and, if desired, pecans. Lightly spray the inside of a standard ice cream scoop with cooking spray. Use the scoop to drop dough onto ungreased cookie sheets. Bake 12 to 17 minutes or until lightly browned. Cool several minutes on cookie sheet before transferring cookies to wire rack to completely cool. Makes two dozen cookies.

Nutritional information per serving: 156.42 cal.; 7.62g total fat; 2.77g protein; 19.94g carb.; 111 mg. sodium

Dietary Exchanges 1bread; 0 fruit/vegetable; 0 protein; .7 fat

CHUNKY CHOCOLATE MELT COOKIES

1 cup unbleached white flour, plus 3/4 cup oat flour
3/4 teaspoon baking soda
1/4 teaspoon salt
3/4 cup soy margarine or vegetable shortening
1 cup natural sugar
1 organic egg
1 teaspoon vanilla extract
6 ounces semi-sweetened chocolate chunks, broken into bits or carob chips
3/4 cup finely chopped pecans

Preheat oven to 375 degrees. Combine flour, baking soda, and salt in a medium bowl; set aside. Using an electric mixer on medium speed, cream margarine and sugar. Add egg substitute and vanilla extract. Mix well. Gradually beat in flour mixture; stir in chocolate bits and nuts if desired.

Lightly coat the inside of a standard ice cream scoop cooking spray, and use the scoop to drop dough on ungreased cookie sheet. Bake 12 to 15 minutes until cookies lightly brown. Cool several minutes on cookie sheet. Makes two dozen cookies.

Nutritional information per serving:177.76 cal.; 7.14 total g. fat; 26.79 g. carb.; 144 mg. sodium

Dietary Exchanges 1.75 bread; 0 fruit/vegetable; 0 protein; 1 fat

ALMOND PECAN BISCOTTI

1 1/2 unbleached all-purpose white flour plus 1/2 oat flour
or 2 cups unbleached all-purpose flour
1/2 teaspoon baking powder
1/2 cup buttered flavored vegetable shortening
2/3 cup natural sugar
2 eggs, beaten
1 teaspoon almond extract
1/2 cup finely chopped almonds

Preheat oven to 375 degrees. Lightly grease baking sheet and set aside. Sift flours and baking powder; set aside. With a mixer on medium speed, blend shortening and sugar until well-combined; add eggs and almond extract. Add flour mixture one-third at a time, beating well after each addition. Shape dough into 9-inch logs, placed three-inches apart on prepared baking sheet. Bake for 25 minutes. Remove from oven. And when logs have cooled enough to handle, cut into 1/2-inch slices. Replace slices on baking sheet and bake for 10 minutes. Use a spatula to turn the slices. Bake an additional five minutes. Cool biscotti slices on wire racks. Makes three dozen cookies.

Nutritional information per serving: 80.08 cal.; 4.16g total fat; 1.55g protein 9.09g carb.; 10.31mg. sodium;

Dietary Exchanges .8 bread; 0 fruit/vegetable; 0 protein; .8 fat

SOUTHERN PECAN BISCOTTI

2 cups unbleached all-purpose white flour
plus 3/4 cup oat flour
1 teaspoon baking powder
1/2 cup buttered-flavored vegetable shortening
2/3 cup natural sugar
Egg substitute equivalent to 2 eggs or 2 organic eggs
1 1/4 cup unbleached all-purpose white flour
2 teaspoons vanilla extract
1/2 cup finely chopped nuts

Preheat oven to 375 degrees. Lightly grease baking sheet and set aside. Sift flours with baking powder; set aside. With a mixer on medium speed, blend shortening and sugar until well-combined; add eggs, vanilla extract, and nuts. Add sifted flour mixture by the spoonful, beating well after each addition. Shape dough into 9-inch logs, placed three-inches apart on prepared baking sheet. Bake for 25 minutes. Remove from oven. And when logs have cooled enough to handle, cut into 1/2-inch slices. Replace slices on baking sheet, and bake for 10 minutes. Use a spatula to turn the slices. Bake an additional five minutes. Cool biscotti slices on wire racks. Makes three dozen cookies

Nutritional information per serving: 79.84 cal.; 4.42 total g. fat; 1.32g. protein 8.84 g. carb.; 17.12 mg. sodium;
Dietary Exchanges .5 bread; 0 fruit/vegetable; 0 protein; .8 fat

SUGAR COOKIES

1 1/3 cup all- purpose unbleached white flour
3/4 vegetable shortening
3/4 cup natural sugar, plus 2 tablespoons
2 organic eggs
1 teaspoon vanilla extract
1/4 teaspoon salt (*optional*)

Preheat oven to 375 degrees. Using a mixer set on medium speed, beat shortening for 30 seconds. Add 3/4 cup sugar; beat until combined. Beat in eggs and vanilla. Add flour and salt (if desired). Use the mixer at first until batter becomes too stiff. Use a wooden spoon to stir in remaining flour. Shape dough into 1-inch balls. Roll balls in remaining sugar before placing them 2-inches apart on an ungreased baking sheet. Bake for seven to eight minutes until lightly browned. Transfer cookies to a wire rack to cool. Makes 24 cookies.

Nutritional information per serving: 100.91 cal.; 2.28g total fat; 1.36g protein17.18g carb.; 5.34mg. sodium;
Dietary Exchanges .7 bread; 0 fruit/vegetable; 0 protein;1.3 fat

BETTER THAN
FUDGE BROWNIES

2 bars (2 ounces each) unsweetened baking chocolate
3/4 cups natural sugar
1/2 stick soy margarine, at room temperature
1/2 cup warm water
1 cup unbleached all-purpose white flour
1/3 cup of wheat or oat flour
2 organic eggs, beaten
2 teaspoons vanilla extract
1/2 teaspoon baking soda
3/4 cups walnuts (optional)

Preheat oven to 350 degrees. Prepare a baking dish with cooking spray and set aside. Break up baking chocolate into bits; set aside. Sift flour and baking soda; set aside. Over medium heat, combine sugar and margarine in a medium saucepan. Reduce heat to low; stir in water. Bring mixture to a boil and immediately remove from heat. Add chopped chocolate, and stir until chocolate melts. Let mixture rest for one minute before slowly whisking in a tablespoon of beaten egg into chocolate mixture. Repeat with an additional tablespoon of egg. Whisk this mixture into chocolate and whisk in remaining beaten egg.

Add vanilla extract, followed by sifted flour mixture. The batter will be thick. Using a large wooden spoon, add nuts. Spread mixture into a prepared 13-by-9-by-2-inch baking pan.

Bake for 20 minutes. Allow brownies to cool in pan before cutting into squares. Makes two dozen brownies.

Nutritional information per serving: 94.71 cal.;3.54g total fat; 2.62 g. protein; 13.67 g. carb.; 53.98mg. sodium;

Dietary Exchanges .8 bread; 0 fruit/vegetable; 0 protein; .5 fat

TEA CAKES

3 cups of unbleached all purpose white flour
2 teaspoons baking powder
1 teaspoon nutmeg
1/2 teaspoon cinnamon
1/2 cup soy margarine, melted
1 cup sugar
2 organic egg beaten
2 teaspoons vanilla extract
2 tablespoons soymilk (*optional*)

Preheat oven to 375 degrees. In a medium bowl mix flour, baking powder, nutmeg, and cinnamon; set aside. Cut the shortening into the flour mixture until it resembles crumbs; set aside. Using a mixer on medium speed, cream sugar, egg and vanilla. Blend in flour mixture by spoonfuls. Drop dough by rounded teaspoons 2 inches apart on baking sheet. Bake 8-10 minutes until cookie edges begin to lightly brown. Cool on cookie sheet for several minutes before transferring to wire rack to cool completely. Makes approximately two dozen cookies.

Nutritional information per serving: 151 cal.; 6.83g total fat; 1.92g protein; 20.43g carb.; 108 mg. sodium

Dietary Exchanges 1.2 bread; 0 fruit/vegetable; 0 protein; 1.3 fat

BETTER THAN BUTTER COOKIES

2 1/2 cups unbleached all-purpose white flour
1 teaspoon baking soda
1/2 teaspoon baking powder
1/4 teaspoon salt (*optional*)
1/2 cup soy butter
2/3 cup of natural sugar
2 organic eggs, beaten
1- 8 ounce carton sour cream
2 teaspoons soy milk
1 teaspoon vanilla extract
3/4 cup walnuts

Preheat oven to 350 degrees. Prepare a baking dish with cooking spray; set aside. Sift flour, baking powder, baking soda, and optional salt; set aside. With an electric mixer on medium speed, blend butter, sugar, eggs, sour cream, soy milk, and vanilla extract until creamy. Stir in walnuts. Drop dough by rounded teaspoons 2-inches apart on baking sheet. Bake approximately 10 minutes or until edges begin to brown. Transfer cookies to a wire rack to cool. Makes two dozen cookies.

Nutritional information per serving: 100.91 cal.; 2.28g total fat; 3.18g protein; 17.18 g. carb.; 90.14 mg. sodium;

Dietary Exchanges 1 bread; 0 fruit/vegetable; 0 protein; .3 fat

PEANUT BUTTER COOKIES

1/2 cup organic soy butter
1/2 cup peanut butter
3/4 cup natural sugar
1/2 teaspoon baking powder
1 teaspoon baking soda
Egg substitute equal to 2 eggs, or 2 organic eggs
1 teaspoon vanilla
1 cup unbleached all-purpose white flour
1/4 cup wheat pastry flour

Preheat oven to 375 degrees. Using a mixer on medium speed, beat butter and peanut butter for 30 seconds. Add sugar, baking powder and baking soda. Beat well, stopping mixer to scrape sides of bowl as necessary. Beat in egg substitute and vanilla extract until well-combined. Beat in as much of the flour as the mixer can handle. Using a wooden spoon, stir in any remaining flour. If necessary, cover and chill dough to make it easy to shape into one -inch balls. Arrange balls 2 inches apart on an ungreased cookie sheet. Flatten by making crisscross marks with the tines of a fork. Bake for seven to nine minutes or until cookie bottoms are lightly browned. Transfer cookies to a wire rack to cool. Makes two dozen cookies.

Nutritional information per serving: 109.65 cal.; 4.63g total fat; 2.77g protein; 13.95g carb.; 119 mg. sodium
Dietary Exchanges: .8 bread; 0 fruit/vegetable; 0 protein; 1.4 fat

TIS' THE SEASON COOKIE

1/2 cup vegetable shortening
1/4 cup natural sugar
1 egg, beaten
1 teaspoon vanilla extract
1 cup unbleached all-purpose flour
1 cup of chopped almonds or pecans
3/4 cups of strawberry jelly

Preheat oven to 350 degrees. With a mixer on medium speed, cream shortening and sugar. Blend in egg, vanilla extract, and chopped almonds or pecans. Spoon flour into creamed mixture. Refrigerate dough for 30 minutes. Form dough into 1-inch balls and place on ungreased cookie sheet. Indent the dough using the back of a measuring spoon designed to measure one teaspoon. Use your fingertip or the back of a spoon to make indentions in the dough. Place a small dab of jelly into each cookie indention. Bake cookies for 12-15 minutes. Remove baking pans from oven; let cookies cool for several minutes on cookie sheet before transferring to wire rack to completely cool. Makes two dozen cookies.

Nutritional information per serving: 131.47 cal.; 7.88g total fat; 1.20g protein; 14.01g carb.; 7.82 mg. sodium
Dietary Exchanges .9 bread; 0 fruit/vegetable; 0 protein; 1.5 fat

Pies, puddi

AN ANGEL GETS HIS APPOINTMENT TO PIE HEAVEN.

I was raised in rural Yazoo and Holmes County, Mississippi, and moved several times during my childhood. Regardless of where we lived, there was always a large fruit orchard filled with red delicious apples, granny apples, yellow apples, peaches, pears, plums, muscadines and blackberries. Mom would send us out after the morning dew had dried to pick fruit for canning and for making pies and cobblers. In retrospect, as a child, I was blessed to be able to climb trees, pick fruits and help my mother and sisters prepare those fruits for the winter months when the vines and branches would become bare.

ngs & crusts

God must have known how poor we were, and He provided for us then as He provides for us now.

I enjoyed picking fruit. My mother taught us early how to select fruit for canning and for making fresh pies. My mother made the best pies. One could smell them a mile away. Her crusts were so thin and flaky that they seemed to melt in your mouth. As I modified her pie recipes, I felt overwhelmed by the memories that they evoked.

People came from near and far to taste my mom's sweet potato pie. I think that we all had our favorite pie, and, for some of us, every pie was a favorite. By now you know that my parents gave birth to seven daughters and one son. Johnathan was the youngest of the crew and the lover of all pies, especially mom's sweet potato pie. I think my mom always made it extra special for him, and although he is no longer with us, I know that he is in pie heaven encouraging me to go that extra mile to create another great pie recipe.

As I selected my fruit and prepared my crust, I hoped that my Naturally Yours pies would reflect my mother's years of labor. After testing my pies she was tickled and said, "Baby, these are better than the ones I make, and they are lighter too."

SOUTHERN-STYLE
APPLE PIE

**5 cups peeled,
cored and sliced Granny Smith apples
3/4 cup natural sugar,
reserve 1 teaspoon
3 tablespoons unbleached white flour
1 teaspoon ground cinnamon
2 teaspoons soy butter or organic unsalted butter, cut into 4 parts
2 (9-inch) unbaked pie crusts, made with
whole-wheat or unbleached white flour**

Preheat oven to 375 degrees. Line a prepared pie pan with crust. In a large bowl, combine apples, natural sugar (reserving 1 teaspoon), flour, cinnamon, and nutmeg; stir to coat apple slices. Let filling stand for 10 minutes before spooning over bottom crust. Top apples with soy butter parts before adding second crust. Trim edges and cut 3 slits in the top pie crust to allow steam to escape. Dust crust with 1 teaspoon of sugar. Bake at 375 degrees for 50 minutes. Cool on wire rack. Makes 8 servings.

Nutritional information per serving: cal.; total g. fat; g. carb.; 241 mg. sodium

Dietary Exchanges 2.5 bread; 1 fruit/vegetable; 0 protein; 2 fat

SINGLE CRUST SOUTHERN-STYLE APPLE PIE

5 cups peeled, cored and sliced Granny Smith apples
3/4 cup of natural sugar
3 tablespoons unbleached flour
1 teaspoon ground cinnamon
2 teaspoons soy butter or organic unsalted butter, cut into 4 parts
1 (9-inch) unbaked pie crust, made with whole-wheat or unbleached flour

Preheat oven to 375 degrees. Line a prepared pie pan with crust. In a large bowl, combine apples, natural sugar, flour, cinnamon, and nutmeg, stirring to completely coat apple slices. Let filling stand for 10 minutes before topping crust with filling. Dust with natural sugar. Bake at 375 degrees for 50 minutes. Cool on wire rack. Makes 8 servings.

• Cook's Health Note: An additional 9-inch unbaked pie crust can be used to top filling. Cut 3 slits in the top of the pie crust. (optional)

Nutritional information per serving: 318.11 cal.; 12g total fat; 2.88g protein; 51.51g carb.; 224mg sodium

Dietary Exchanges 2.2 bread; 1.0 fruit/vegetable; .64 protein; 2.85 fat

BLACKBERRY PIE

4 cups fresh or frozen blackberries
3/4 cup natural sugar, reserve 1 teaspoon
2 tablespoons unbleached white flour
2 teaspoons soy butter, cut into 4 parts
1 (9- inch) unbaked pie crust, made with whole-wheat or unbleached white flour

Mix blackberries and sugar in a large bowl, and let berries stand for 15 minutes. Meanwhile, line a prepared 9-inch pie pan with crust; set it aside.

Gently fold flour into blackberries. Spoon berries into pastry crust. Top filling with soy butter parts; dust pie with reserved teaspoon of sugar. Bake at 375 degrees for 50 minutes. Cool on wire rack. Makes 8 servings.

• Cook's Health Note: An additional 9-inch unbaked pie crust can be used to top filling. Cut 3 slits in the top of the pie crust. (optional)

Nutritional information per serving: 247.5 cal.; 8.97 total g. fat; 47.18 g. carb.; 163.23 mg. sodium

Dietary Exchanges 2 bread; 1 fruit/vegetable; 0 protein; 1.5 fat

SWEET POTATO PIE

1 large baked, peeled, mashed sweet potato
1/3 cup natural sugar
1/2 cup soy butter or soy margarine, softened
2 organic eggs
1 teaspoon ground cinnamon
1 teaspoon ground nutmeg
1/4 teaspoon salt
2 teaspoons corn starch
1/2 cup vanilla soymilk
1 unbaked 9-inch pie crust, made with whole wheat flour

Preheat oven to 325 degrees. Line a prepared pie pan with crust; set aside. Combine sweet potato, natural sugar, soy butter, egg substitute, cinnamon, nutmeg, and salt in a large mixing bowl. With an electric mixer on medium speed, beat potato mixture until light and fluffy. Slowly blend in soymilk. Pour mixture into prepared pie shell and bake for 20 minutes. Increase oven temperature to 375 degrees and bake an additional 45 to 50 minutes or until set. Cool before cutting into slices Makes 10 servings.

Nutritional information per serving: 289 cal.; 9.78 total g. fat; 44.36 g. carb.; 313 mg. sodium

Dietary Exchanges 3 bread; 0 fruit/vegetable; .5 protein; 1.5 fat

DANG GOOD PIE

3/4 stick margarine, melted
3/4 cup natural sugar
Egg substitute equal to 3 eggs
1 cup crushed canned unsweetened pineapple, drained
1 cup unsweetened coconut flakes
3 tablespoons unbleached white flour
1 (9-inch) unbaked pastry shell, made with unbleached white flour or whole-wheat flour

Preheat oven to 350 degrees. Combine ingredients in order listed. Pour filling into unbaked pie shell. Bake for 1 hour or until filling is set and golden brown. Makes eight servings.

Nutritional information per serving: 448cal.;20.71 total g. fat; g. carb.; 290 mg. sodium

Dietary Exchanges 2 bread; 0 fruit/vegetable; 1 protein; 1.5 fat

GOOD OLE COCONUT PIE

1/2 cup natural sugar
1/2 cup margarine
2 eggs, beaten
1 cup soymilk
4-ounces frozen or fresh unsweetened coconut flakes
1 teaspoon vanilla extract
1/2 cup unbleached all-purpose white flour
1 9-inch pie shell made from unbleached all-purpose white flour or whole wheat flour

Preheat oven to 325 degrees. With a mixer on medium speed, blend sugar and margarine. Combine until creamy and fluffy. Add eggs, one at a time, beating well after each addition. Blend in soymilk, coconut, vanilla extract, and flour. Pour filling into pie crust. Bake for 40 minutes until filling is firm. Continue baking for an additional 10 minutes or until filling is ready. Remove from oven. Cool on wire rack. Makes 12 servings.

Nutritional information per serving: 252.37cal.; total 13.46 g. fat; 27.35g. carb.; 152.23mg. sodium

Dietary Exchanges 1.6bread; 0 fruit/vegetable; .4 protein; 2.3fat

PUMPKIN PIE

1 (16-ounce) can solid-pack pumpkin, do not use pumpkin pie mix
2/3 cup natural sugar
Egg substitute equal to 3 eggs, slightly beaten
1 teaspoon ground cinnamon
1 teaspoon ground nutmeg
2 teaspoons vanilla
2 teaspoons of cornstarch
1 cup, plus 2 tablespoons vanilla soymilk
1 unbaked 9-inch pie crust, made with whole wheat flour

Preheat oven to 325 degrees. Line a prepared pie pan with crust; set aside. Combine pumpkin, sugar, egg substitute, spices, and salt in a large mixer bowl. With an electric mixer at medium speed, beat pumpkin mixture until light and fluffy. Add cornstarch; slowly blend in soy milk. Spoon mixture into prepared pie shell and bake for 20 minutes. Increase oven temperature to 375 degrees and bake an additional 45 to 50 minutes until set. Cool before cutting into slices. Makes: 10 servings.

Nutritional information per serving: 157.55 cal.; 5.97 total fat calories; 22.71g carb.; 144.37mg sodium

Dietary Exchanges 1.4 bread; 0 fruit/vegetable; .3 protein; 1.1 fat

PEACH COBBLER PIE

**3 1/2 cups peeled, cored and sliced fresh peaches
or 3 1/2 cups frozen sliced peaches
3/4 cup sugar
2 tablespoons unbleached all-purpose white flour
1 teaspoon ground cinnamon
1 teaspoon ground nutmeg
1 teaspoon vanilla extract
2 (9-inch) unbaked pie crusts, made with whole
wheat or unbleached white flour**

Mix peaches and sugar. Let it stand for 10 minutes. Stir flour, cinnamon, and nutmeg into peach mixture. Add mixture to a medium saucepan and cook over low heat for 10 minutes, stirring often. Add vanilla extract, and pour filling into pie shell. Bake for 50 minutes. Cool on wire rack.

Nutritional information per serving: 334.51cal.; total 13.61 g. fat; 50.12g. carb.; 308.29mg. sodium

Dietary Exchanges 2.5bread; .5 fruit/vegetable; 0 protein; 2.6fat

BAKED RICE PUDDING

**2 eggs or egg substitutes equal to 2 eggs
2 cups vanilla soymilk
1/2 cup natural sugar
2 teaspoons vanilla extract
3 tablespoons butter, melted
1 teaspoon ground nutmeg
1 teaspoon ground cinnamon
1/4 cup soy butter or margarine
1 1/2 cups prepared white rice, or 1 1/2 cups prepared brown rice
3/4 cup raisins**

Preheat oven to 325 degrees. Using a mixer on medium speed, combine eggs, milk, sugar, vanilla extract and salt. Blend in melted butter, nutmeg, cinnamon and raisins. Mix with prepared rice and spoon batter into a 13-by-9-inch greased baking pan.

Bake for 30 minutes, or until a knife inserted near the center comes out clean.

Nutritional information per serving: 138.05cal.; total 3.03 g. fat; 24.52g. carb.; 33.16mg. sodium

Dietary Exchanges 1.1 bread; .4 fruit/vegetable; . protein; .5fat

MORNING
BANANA PUDDING

1/2 cup natural sugar
3 egg whites
3 egg yolks
3 cups vanilla soymilk
3 teaspoons vanilla extract
2 teaspoons lemon extract
30 natural vanilla-wafer-style cookies,
such as MI-Del Vanilla Snaps
5 medium ripe bananas

Preheat oven to 350 degrees. Blend 1/2 cup of sugar and 3 egg yolks until sugar dissolves. Stir in soymilk and place mixture in a double-boiler or heavy pot. Cook for 15 minutes, stirring until custard thickens; add extracts. Layer cookies in the bottom 8-by-11-by-2-inch baking dish. Peel bananas as needed to add a layer of banana slices over cookies. Top with another layer of cookies and continue layering bananas and cookies. Finish with a cookie layer. Pour custard over layers. Set aside.

Prepare meringue by beating egg whites until whites form firm peaks. Add sugar and extracts; beat up to one additional minute to form thick glossy meringue. Spread meringue over banana and cookie layers. Brown in oven for three to five minutes; no longer than five minutes.

Nutritional information per serving: cal.; total g. fat; g. carb.; 55 mg. sodium Dietary Exchanges 1.5 bread; .5 fruit/vegetable; .5 protein; 0 fat

DOUBLE FUDGE PIE

1/2 cup flour
2 tablespoons Dutch-processed cocoa
1/2 cup natural sugar
1/2 cup soy or organic butter
egg substitutes equal to 2 eggs or 2 organic eggs
1/2 cup walnuts, optional
1 9-inch pie shell

Preheat oven to 325 degrees. Sift flour with cocoa; set aside. With a mixer on medium speed, blend sugar and butter until creamy and fluffy. Add egg substitute slowly, beating well after each addition. Add pecans. Pour filling into a greased 9-inch pie pan. Bake for 25 minutes. Cool on wire rack. Makes 12 servings.

Nutritional information per serving: 175.01cal.; total 5.79 g. fat; 24.69g. carb.; 94.84 mg. sodium

Dietary Exchanges 1.5 bread; 0 fruit/vegetable; .6 protein; .9 fat

OLD-FASHIONED BREAD PUDDING

3 (6-ounce) slices wheat or oat bread
2 1/4 cups vanilla soymilk mixed with
2 tablespoons cider vinegar
2 organic eggs, plus 1 egg substitute, or 3 organic eggs, beaten slightly
2/3 cup natural sugar
1/2 cup raisins
2 tablespoons vanilla extract
3 tablespoons soy butter or margarine, melted

Preheat oven at 325 degrees. Cut wheat rolls in half and place on a cookie sheet. Bake five to 10 minutes or until bread dries and hardens. Cool on wire racks.

Break bread into small chunks and place them in a large bowl. Add milk; soak for approximately 10 minutes. Crush bread with hands until blended with the milk. Add eggs, sugar, raisins, and vanilla extract. Spoon mixture into nine 3-by-5-mini-pans. Top with melted butter. Bake for 40 to 50 minutes or until pudding firms.

Cool pans on wire racks. Makes 12 to 15 servings.

Nutritional information per serving: 285.82cal.; total 7.53 g. fat; 46.08g. carb.; 349.45mg. sodium

Dietary Exchanges 2.4 bread; .7 fruit/vegetable; protein; 1.0fat

CUSTARD PIE

1/3 cup natural sugar
1 teaspoon nutmeg
4 organic eggs
2 cups soymilk
1 teaspoon ground nutmeg
2 teaspoons vanilla extract
1 9-inch prepared wheat crust pie crust

Preheat oven to 400 degrees. Place prepared pie crust in a pie pan. Prick the dough several times with a fork. Place a buttered piece of foil face down onto the pastry, and line the unbuttered side with dried beans. Bake for three to five minutes. When cool enough to handle, remove foil-lined beans from pie crust.

To make filling: Combine sugar, nutmeg and flour in a mixer bowl. Using a mixer on low speed, add eggs slowly, beating well after each addition until well blended. Stir in soymilk, melted butter, lemon juice, and vanilla. Cover edge or piecrust with foil to prevent over-browning. Pour filling into crust. Bake at 350 degrees for 50 minutes.

• Cook's note: Use dry beans as a weight.

Nutritional information per serving: 186.05cal.; total 9.48 g. fat; 20.06g. carb.; 159.36mg. sodium
Dietary Exchanges 1.2 bread; .0 fruit/vegetable; .0 protein; 1.7fat

CHESS PIE

1 cup natural sugar
2 tablespoons unbleached cornmeal
4 organic eggs
1/2 cup of soymilk
2 teaspoons lemon juice
1/4 cup soy margarine, melted and cooled
1/8 cup lemon juice
1 tablespoon finely shredded lemon peel
1 teaspoon vanilla
1 9-inch prepared wheat crust/ pie crust

Preheat oven to 350 degrees. Line a 9 inch pie pan crust. Prick the dough several times with a fork. Place a buttered piece of foil face down onto the pastry, and line the unbuttered side with dried beans. Bake for three to five minutes. When cool enough to handle, remove foil-lined beans from pie crust.

Combine sugar and cornmeal; and set aside. Combine soymilk, lemon juice, lemon zest; set aside. Beat eggs with a mixer on medium speed. Stir in sugar, cornmeal, soymilk mixture, melted margarine, and vanilla extract.

To prevent the edge of pie from over browning, place an edging of foil around the rim of crust. Bake for 50 minutes.

• Cook's note: Use dry beans as a weight.

Nutritional information per serving: 297.92cal.; total 11.52 g. fat; 41.45g. carb.; 228.47mg. sodium
Dietary Exchanges 1.2 bread; .0 fruit/vegetable; .0 protein; 1.7fat

SINGLE PIECRUST

1 cup unbleached all-purpose white flour
2 tablespoons vegetable shortening, chilled
3 tablespoons cold water
1/4 teaspoon salt

Place flour and salt in a medium bowl. Cut shortening into the flour mixture until it resembles coarse crumbs. Drizzle a small amount of water over a portion of the flour mix and use a fork to blend with flour. Add remaining water and form dough into a ball. Do not overwork. Place dough on lightly floured surface and knead until smooth. Place dough on a floured surface and roll out to fit 9-inch pie pan. Makes six or eight servings.

Nutritional information per six servings: 118.6 cal.; 4.52g fat; 2.53g protein; 16.67g carb.; 97.12 mg. sodium
Dietary Exchanges 1 bread; 0 fruit/vegetable; 0 protein; .8 fat
Nutritional information per eight servings: 89.56 cal.; 3.39g fat; 189g protein; 12.5g carb.; 72.84 mg. sodium
Dietary Exchanges .8 bread; 0 fruit/vegetable; 0 protein; .6 fat

DOUBLE PIECRUST

2 cups unbleached all-purpose white flour
4 tablespoons vegetable shortening, chilled
5 to 6 tablespoons cold water
1/4 teaspoon salt

Place flour and salt in a medium bowl. Cut shortening into the flour mixture until it resembles coarse crumbs. Drizzle a small amount of water over a portion of the flour mix and use a fork to blend with flour. Add remaining water and form dough into a ball. Cover a little less than half of dough with plastic; refrigerate. Place the larger section on a lightly floured surface; knead until smooth. Roll out dough on a floured surface to fit a 9-inch pie pan. Place in pan and prick the bottom crust with the tines of a fork in several places.

When ready to top filling with second crust, remove remaining dough from refrigerator. Knead until smooth and roll out in circle. Makes six or eight servings.

Nutritional information per six servings: 237.12 cal.; 9.05g fat; 5.05g protein; 33.33g carb.; 97.30 mg. sodium
Dietary Exchanges 2 bread; 0 fruit/vegetable; 0 protein; 1.7 fat
Nutritional information per eight servings: 177.84 cal.; 6.79g fat; 3.79g protein; 25g carb.; 72.98 mg. sodium

SINGLE WHOLE WHEAT PIE CRUST

1/2 cup whole wheat flour
1/2 cup unbleached all-purpose white flour
3 tablespoons vegetable shortening, chilled
4 tablespoons cold water

Place flour and salt in a medium bowl. Cut shortening into the flour mixture until it resembles coarse crumbs. Drizzle a small amount of water over a portion of the flour mix and use a fork to blend with flour. Add remaining water and form dough into a ball. Place the dough on a lightly floured surface; knead until smooth. Roll out dough on floured surface to fit a 9-inch pie pan. Place in pie pan, and prick the bottom crust with the tines of a fork in several places. Makes six servings.

Nutritional information per six servings: 131 cal.; 6.79g fat; 2.63g protein; 15.59g carb.; .80 mg. sodium
Dietary Exchanges .9 bread; 0 fruit/vegetable; 0 protein; 1.3 fat
Nutritional information per eight servings: 98.2 cal.; 5.04g fat; 1.97g protein; 11.70g carb.; .60 mg. sodium
Dietary Exchanges: .7 bread; 0 fruit/vegetable; 0 protein; 1 fat

SINGLE NATURAL GRAIN PIE CRUST

1/2 cup whole wheat pastry flour
1/2 cup oat flour
1/2 teaspoon salt
3 tablespoons vegetable shortening, chilled
4 tablespoons cold water

Place flour and salt in a medium bowl. Cut shortening into the flour mixture until it resembles coarse crumbs. Drizzle a small amount of water over a portion of the flour mix and use a fork to blend with flour. Add remaining water and form dough into a ball. Do not overwork. Place dough on lightly floured surface and knead until smooth. Place dough on a floured surface and roll out to fit 9-inch pie pan. Makes six servings.

Nutritional information per six serving: 112.19 cal.; 10.61g total fat; 2.27g protein 7.04g carb.; 194 mg. sodium
Dietary Exchanges .7 bread; 0 fruit/vegetable; 0 protein; 1.3 fat
Nutritional information per eight servings: 84.14 cal.; 5.28g total fat; 1.70g protein; 7.95g carb.; 145.56 mg. sodium
Dietary Exchanges: .5 bread; 0 fruit/vegetable; 0 protein; .9 fat

HONEY GRAHAM SPRINGFORM CRUST

2 cups crushed graham crackers
2 tablespoons natural sugar
3/4 stick soy margarine or organic unsalted butter, melted
1 teaspoon ground cinnamon

Combine all ingredients, mixing well. Firmly press crumb mixture evenly over bottom and sides of a 10-inch springform pan. Bake at 325 degrees for 10 minutes. Makes 12 servings.

Nutritional information per eight servings: 197.65 cal.; 6.79g total fat; 4.37g protein; 30.14g carb.; 231 mg. sodium

Dietary Exchanges: 2 bread; 0 fruit/vegetable; 0 protein; .7 fat

Nutritional information per 12 servings: 131.77 cal.; 4.53g total fat; 2.91g protein; 20.09g carb.; 154 mg. sodium

Dietary Exchanges:1.3 bread; 0 fruit/vegetable; .3 protein; .5 fat

HONEY GRAHAM PIECRUST

1 1/2 cups crushed graham crackers
1 tablespoon natural sugar
1/3 cup soy margarine or organic unsalted butter

Combine all ingredients until well mixed. Firmly press mixture evenly over bottom and sides of a 9-inch pie plate. Bake at 325 degrees for 10 minutes. Makes six or eight servings.

Nutritional information per six serving: 199.32 cal.; 7.20g total fat; 4.61g protein; 29.29g carb.; 236.35 mg. sodium

Dietary Exchanges 1.9 bread; 0 fruit/vegetable; 0 protein; .8 fat

Nutritional information per eight servings:149.49 cal.; 6.40g total fat; 3.46g protein; 21.96g carb.; 236.35 mg. sodium

Dietary Exchanges: 1.9 bread; 0 fruit/vegetable; 0 protein; 8 fat

NATURAL VANILLA WAFER CRUST

2 cups crushed vanilla wafers
3/4 stick of soy margarine
or organic unsalted butter, melted

Combine all ingredients until well mixed. Firmly press mixture evenly over bottom and sides of a 10-inch springform pan. Bake at 325 degrees for 10 minutes. Makes 12 servings.

Nutritional information per serving: 217.41 cal.; 8.07g total fat; 3.15g protein; 29.37g carb.; 148.57 mg. sodium

Dietary Exchanges: 2.5 bread; 0 fruit/vegetable; 0 protein; 1.1 fat

NATURAL VANILLA WAFER PIE CRUST

1 1/2 cups crushed vanilla wafers
1 tablespoon natural sugar
1/3 cup soy margarine
or organic unsalted butter, melted

Combine all ingredients until well mixed. Firmly press mixture evenly over bottom and sides of a 10-inch springform pan. Bake at 325 degrees for 10 minutes. Makes 10 servings.

Nutritional information per serving: 200.99 cal.; 8.07g total fat; 2.74g protein; 30.76g carb.; 142.53 mg. sodium

Dietary Exchanges 2.5 bread; 0 fruit/vegetable; 0 protein; 1.1 fat

Frozen deligh

NO ONE KNEW ABOUT MY SECRET LOVE FOR A MAN AT LEAST 30 YEARS OLDER THAN ME, WHO GAVE ME SO MUCH JOY.

Ice cream was a great thing in the summer time. I do not know where you grew up, but it was really hot in Mississippi with plenty of cotton fields and no air conditioners. My mother always watched the news at noon to determine the weather for the next day. For a sharecropper, the weather determined your workday. My mother always had a spring and fall garden, and she took her planting cue from the weatherman. Even as a child, the weatherman became an important factor in my life. Not because he reported the weather for the day, but because he did an ice cream commercial for a brand name ice cream company. Woody Assaf, the weatherman, would have ice cream in a large glass serving dish. He would take a large spoon and place it in his mouth

ts ice creams

and make this "hmmmm" sound to indicate how good it was. Each day he would eat a different flavor. I could not wait until I grew up so that I could be just like the weatherman and experience a different flavor each day. I loved Woody Assaf.

The Fourth of July was always a fun holiday! My uncles would come from Chicago, and they would buy boxes of ice cream. I would try to eat enough ice cream to last until they came the following summer. My mother would make ice cream on the Fourth of July. She prepared the custard on the stove, and it seemed like she cooked it forever. At last, she poured the custard in the can and placed it in the ice cream bucket. My sisters and I took turns churning the ice cream, and my mother would check on it until it acquired her desired thickness. When it was ready, we all got a half a cup of ice cream. I would pray that people would not show up so I could get another serving. Sometimes I was lucky, but most times I was not.

Well, life has changed a lot since then. I no longer churn ice cream; I use a blender and an electric ice cream maker instead. I have luscious creamy ice cream within 30 minutes. My mother has tested my ice cream recipe, and she loves it!

I have found a healthy way to fulfill my childhood dream of having ice cream every day, and I can even have a different flavor to enchance the excitement. The best part about it—healthy is just as delicious! Each time I spoon up my favorite ice cream, I give a toast to my friend, Woody Assaf.

VANILLA ICE CREAM DELIGHT

**2 cups vanilla soymilk,
rice milk or skim milk, chilled
1(12.3-ounce) box firm silken tofu
6-ounce Neufchatel cheese
3/4 cup natural sugar
2 teaspoons vanilla extract**

Place all ingredients in a blender
or food processor container. Process
until smooth; pour into ice cream
freezer container. Freeze according to
manufacturer's instructions. Makes 8
servings.

*Nutritional information per serving:
153.13 cal.; 6.11g total fat; .75g protein 19.89g carb.; 110mg sodium*

*Dietary Exchanges 1 bread; 0 fruit/
vegetable; .75 protein; 1fat*

NON-DAIRY FROZEN VANILLA
ICE CREAM DELIGHT

**2 cups vanilla soymilk
1 (12.3-ounce) box firm silken tofu, chilled
8-ounces non-dairy cream cheese substitute
2 tablespoons canola oil
3/4 cup natural sugar
2 teaspoons vanilla extract**

Place all ingredients in a blender or
food processor container. Process
until smooth; pour into ice cream
freezer container. Freeze according
to manufacturer's instructions. Makes
8 servings.

*Nutritional information per serving:
154.45 cal.; 6.25g total fat; 5.4 g protein 18.95g carb.; 120.65mg sodium*

*Dietary Exchanges .9 bread; .6 fruit/
vegetable; 5.4 protein; 1 fat*

54

CHOCOLATE LOVER'S DREAM ICE CREAM

2 cups soymilk, rice milk or lowfat milk, chilled
1(12.3 ounce) box firm silken tofu, chilled
6-ounces Neufchatel cheese
1 (1-ounce) packet of pre-melted unsweetened chocolate
2 tablespoons unsweetened Dutch-process cocoa
3/4 cup natural sugar
1 teaspoon vanilla extract
1 teaspoon lemon extract

Place all ingredients in a blender or food processor container. Process until smooth; pour into ice cream freezer container. Freeze according to manufacturer's instructions. Makes 8 servings.

• Cook's note: Use canola oil only when this mixture is prepared with a non-dairy cream cheese substitute. Do not add oil when using Neufchatel cheese.

Nutritional information per serving: 151.25 cal.; 6.71g total fat;5.6g protein; 19.64g carb.; 79mg sodium

Dietary Exchanges .7 bread; .2 fruit/vegetable; .6 protein; 1.4 fat

CHOCOLATE LOVER'S NON-DAIRY DREAM ICE CREAM

2 cups soymilk, chilled
1 (12.3-ounce) box firm silken tofu
8-ounces non-dairy cream cheese substitute
1 (1-ounce) packet of pre-melted unsweetened chocolate
2 tablespoons unsweetened Dutch-process cocoa
1 teaspoon canola oil
1/2 cup natural sugar
1 teaspoon vanilla extract
1 teaspoon lemon extract

Place all ingredients in a blender or food processor container. Process until smooth; pour into ice cream freezer container. Freeze according to manufacturer's instructions. Makes one quart.

Nutritional information per serving: 162.17 cal.; 9.08 total grams fat; .4.28g protein 16.79g carb.; 188.84 mg. sodium

Dietary Exchanges .7 bread; 0 fruit/vegetable; .4 protein; 1 fat

CHERRY DREAM CREAM DELIGHT

2 cups vanilla soymilk, rice milk or skim milk, chilled
6-ounces non-dairy cream cheese substitute
or 6-ounces Neufchatel cheese
1 (12.3-ounce) box of firm silken tofu
1 tablespoon canola oil, see note
3/4 cup natural sugar
2 teaspoons vanilla extract
3/4 cup frozen or fresh cherries with seeds removed

Place all ingredients in a blender or food processor container. Process until smooth; pour into ice cream freezer container. Freeze according to manufacturer's instructions. Makes 12 servings.

• Cook's note: Use canola oil only when this mixture is prepared with a non-dairy cream cheese substitute. Do not add oil when using Neufchatel cheese.

Nutritional information per serving: 140 cal.; 4.54g total fat; 4.52g protein 20.81g carb.;84.39 mg sodium

Dietary Exchanges .9 bread; 0 fruit/vegetable; .5 protein; .7 fat

BETTER THAN BANANA PUDDING FREEZE

2 cups vanilla soymilk, rice milk or skim milk, chilled
8-ounces non-dairy cream cheese substitute
1 (12.3-ounce) box firm silken tofu
1 tablespoon canola oil, see note
3/4 cup natural sugar
2 teaspoons banana extract
1/4 teaspoon cinnamon
1 large ripe banana, mashed
1/2 cup crushed natural vanilla wafers, made with organic unbleached wheat flour
1/3 cup crushed pecans (optional)

Place the first eight ingredients in a blender or food processor container. Process until smooth; pour into ice cream freezer container. Freeze according to manufacturer's instructions. Three to five minutes before freezing is complete, add mashed banana, crushed pecans, and natural vanilla wafers to the ice cream freezer container. Complete freezing process. Makes 13 servings.

• Cook's note: Use canola oil only when this mixture is prepared with a non-dairy cream cheese substitute. Do not add oil when using Neufchatel cheese.

Nutritional information per serving:176.71 cal.; 6.03g total fat; 4.52g protein 27.09g carb.;114mg sodium

Dietary Exchanges 1.5 bread; 0 fruit/vegetable; .5 protein; .9fat

MISSISSIPPI ROCKY ROAD CREAM

2 cups vanilla soymilk, rice milk or skim milk, chilled
6-ounces non-dairy cream cheese substitute or
1(12.3 ounces) box firm silken tofu chilled
6-ounces Neufchatel cheese
2 tablespoons canola oil, see note
3/4 cup natural sugar
2 teaspoons vanilla extract
1/2 cup semi-sweet chocolate bits
1/2 cup unsweetened coconut
1/3 cup of finely chopped peanuts or pecans (*optional*)

• Cook's note: Use canola oil only when this mixture is prepared with a non-dairy cream cheese substitute. Do not add oil when using Neufchatel cheese.

Place first six ingredients in a blender or food processor jar. Process until smooth; pour into ice cream freezer container. Freeze according to manufacturer's instructions. Three to five minutes before freezing is complete, add chocolate, coconut, and optional nuts to the freezer container. Complete freezing process. Makes 12 servings.

Nutritional information per serving: 197.72 cal.; 11.41 total fat; 5.67g protein 20.37g carb.; 75.15mg sodium

Dietary Exchanges 1.1 bread; 0 fruit/vegetable; .5 protein; 2 fat

NON-DAIRY EGGNOG ICE CREAM

2 cups vanilla soymilk, chilled
1(12.3 ounces) box firm silken tofu
8-ounces non-dairy cream cheese substitute
1/3 cup egg replacement
2 teaspoons canola oil
1/2 cup natural sugar
1 teaspoon natural yellow food coloring
1 teaspoon ground cinnamon
2 teaspoons ground nutmeg
2 teaspoons vanilla extract

Place all ingredients in a blender or food processor container. Process until smooth; pour into ice cream freezer container. Freeze according to manufacturer's instructions. Makes 8 servings.

Nutritional information per serving: 150.71 cal.; 8.21 total grams fat; 4.75g protein 14.58g carb.; 185.68 mg. sodium

Dietary Exchanges .6 bread; 0 fruit/vegetable; .5 protein; 1.6 fat

ALA' MOCHA ICE CREAM

2 cups vanilla soymilk, rice milk or skim milk, chilled
1 (8-ounce) package Neufchatel cheese or 8-ounces non-dairy cream cheese substitute
2 tablespoons canola oil, see note
2 tablespoons of a coffee alternative (such as Kafree) or decaffeinated coffee
1/3 cup Dutch-processed cocoa or carob powder
3/4 cup natural sugar
2 teaspoons vanilla extract

Place all ingredients in a blender or food processor container. Process until smooth; pour into ice cream freezer container. Freeze according to manufacturer's instructions. Makes one quart.

• Cook's note: Use canola oil only when this mixture is prepared with a non-dairy cream cheese substitute. Do not add oil when using Neufchatel cheese.

Nutritional information per serving: 160.19 cal.; 8.39 total grams fat; 4.54g protein 16.69g carb.; 181.1 mg. sodium

Dietary Exchanges .8 bread; 0 fruit/vegetable; .3 protein; 1.6 fat

NON-DAIRY TUTTI FRUITTI

2 cups vanilla soymilk
1 (12.3 ounce)box firm silken tofu
8-ounces non-dairy cream cheese substitute
2 teaspoons canola oil
1/2 cup natural sugar
1 teaspoon vanilla extract
1 teaspoon almond extract
1/2 cup fresh pineapple, chopped, or 1/2 cup crushed unsweetened pineapple
3 ounces Maraschino green cherries
3 ounces Maraschino red cherries

Rinse cherries and soak in a small bowl of cold water; set aside. Place soymilk, tofu, cream cheese substitute, oil, sugar, extracts, and pineapple in blender or food processor container. Place all ingredients in a blender or food processor container. Process until smooth; pour into ice cream freezer container. Freeze according to manufacturer's instructions. Makes eight servings.

• Cook's note: cherries are soaked in cold water to remove additional sugar and dye before adding to the recipe.

Nutritional information per serving: 138.88 cal.; 7.22 total grams fat; .3.78g protein 15.56g carb.; 139.59 mg. sodium

Dietary Exchanges .6 bread; .4 fruit/vegetable; .3 protein; 1.4 fat

TUTTI FRUITTI

2 cups vanilla soymilk, rice milk
or lowfat milk
1 (12.3-ounce) box firm silken tofu
8-ounces Neufchatel cheese
1/2 cup natural sugar
1 teaspoon vanilla extract
1 teaspoon almond extract
1/2 cup fresh pineapple, chopped or
1/2 cup canned unsweetened crushed pineapple
3 ounces Maraschino green cherries
3 ounces Maraschino red cherries

Rinse cherries and soak in a small bowl of cold water; set aside. Place all ingredients in a blender or food processor container. Process until smooth; pour into ice cream freezer container. Freeze according to manufacturer's instructions. Makes eight servings.

• Cook's note: cherries are soaked in cold water to remove additional sugar and dye before adding to the recipe.

Nutritional information per serving: 128.57 cal.; 5.56g total fat; 5 g protein; 15.95g carb.; 70.83mg sodium

Dietary Exchanges .6 bread; 0 fruit/vegetable; .75 protein; 1fat

CHOCOLATE CHIP COOKIES AND CREAM

2 cups vanilla soy milk, chilled
6-ounces non-dairy cream cheese substitute or 6-ounces Neufchatel cheese
1 (12.3-ounce) box firm silken tofu
1 tablespoon canola oil, see note
3/4 cup natural sugar
1/2 cup of crushed natural chocolate chips
2 teaspoons vanilla extract

Place all ingredients in a blender or food processor container. Process until smooth; pour into ice cream freezer container. Freeze according to manufacturer's instructions. Makes 11 servings.

• Cook's note: Oil is used only when you prepare the mixture with a non-dairy cream cheese substitute. Do not use oil when adding Neufchatel cheese.

Nutritional information per serving:184 cal.; 7.33g total fat; 5.24g protein 25g carb.; 124.30mg sodium

Dietary Exchanges 1.2 bread; 0 fruit/vegetable; .5 protein; 1.2 fat

FANTASY PRALINE CREAM

2 cups vanilla soymilk, rice milk or skim milk, chilled
6-ounces non-dairy cream cheese substitute or 6-ounces Neufchatel cheese
1 (12.3-ounce) box of firm silken tofu
2 tablespoons canola oil, see note
1/2 cup maple syrup
2 teaspoons vanilla butternut extract
1/2 cup crushed pecans

Place all ingredients in a blender or food processor container. Process until smooth; pour into ice cream freezer container. Freeze according to manufacturer's instructions. Makes 11 servings.

• Cook's note: Use canola oil only when this mixture is prepared with a non-dairy cream cheese substitute. Do not add oil when using Neufchatel cheese.

Nutritional information per serving:160 cal.; 8.72g total fat;5.21g protein 16.80g carb.;94.02mg sodium

Dietary Exchanges .7 bread; 0 fruit/vegetable; .6 protein; 1.5fat

GEORGIA PEACHY CREAM

Peach Mixture:
3/4 cup frozen or fresh peach slices
2 tablespoons water
2 teaspoons natural sugar
1 teaspoon soy butter
1/4 teaspoon ground cinnamon
Creamy Mixture:
2 cups vanilla soy milk, rice milk or skim milk,
chilled 6-ounces non-dairy cream cheese substitute
or 6-ounces Neufchatel cheese
1 (12.3-ounce) box of firm silken tofu
2 tablespoons water
1 teaspoon butter
2 tablespoons canola oil, see note
1/2 cup, plus 1 tablespoon natural sugar
2 teaspoons vanilla extract

To prepare peach mixture: Place peach slices in a saucepan with water, two teaspoons of natural sugar, soy butter, and cinnamon. Bring mixture to a boil. Reduce heat and simmer for five minutes. Remove mixture from heat and let cool before chilling for at least two hours.

To prepare creamy mixture: Place ingredients in a blender or food processor container. Process until smooth; pour creamy mixture into an ice cream freezer container. Freeze according to manufacturer's instructions. Three to five minutes before freezing is complete, add chilled peaches to freezer container. Complete freezing process. Makes 11 servings.

• Cook's note: Use canola oil only when this mixture is prepared with a non-dairy cream cheese substitute. Do not add oil when using Neufchatel cheese.

Nutritional information per serving:127.31 cal.; 5.11g total fat; 4.65g protein 16.04g carb.; 92.36mg sodium

Dietary Exchanges .7 bread; 0 fruit/vegetable; .5 protein; .8 fat

LUSCIOUS LEMONY CREAM FREEZE

2 cups vanilla soymilk, rice milk or skim milk, chilled
6-ounces non-dairy cream cheese substitute
or 6-ounces Neufchatel cheese
1 (12.3-ounce) box firm silken tofu
2 tablespoons canola oil, see note
3/4 cup natural sugar
2 teaspoons lemon extract
1/2 teaspoon lemon zest
1/2 teaspoon natural yellow food coloring

Place all ingredients in a blender or food processor container. Process until smooth; pour into ice cream freezer container. Freeze according to manufacturer's instructions. Makes 10 servings.

• Cook's note: Use canola oil only when this mixture is prepared with a non-dairy cream cheese substitute. Do not add oil when using Neufchatel cheese.

Nutritional information per serving:146.4 cal.; 5.27g total fat; 5g protein 20.04g carb.;98.26mg sodium

Dietary Exchanges.1 bread; .6 fruit/vegetable; .9 protein; .8 fat

EGGNOG ICE CREAM

2 cups vanilla soymilk, chilled
1 (12.3-ounce) box firm silken tofu
1 (6-ounce) package Neufchatel cheese
Egg substitute equal to 2 eggs
1/2 cup natural sugar
1 teaspoon natural yellow food coloring
1 teaspoon ground cinnamon
2 teaspoons ground nutmeg
2 teaspoons vanilla extract

Place all ingredients in a blender or food processor container. Process until smooth; pour into ice cream freezer container. Freeze according to manufacturer's instructions. Makes 8 servings.

• Cook's note: Use canola oil only when this mixture is prepared with a non-dairy cream cheese substitute. Do not add oil when using Neufchatel cheese.

Nutritional information per serving: 139.33 cal.; 6.33g total fat; 5.9 g protein; 14.98g carb.; 97.57mg sodium

Dietary Exchanges .7 bread; 0 fruit/vegetable; .7 protein; 1.1 fat

LUSCIOUS LIME CREAM

2 cups vanilla soymilk, rice milk or skim milk, chilled
6-ounces non-dairy cream cheese substitute
or 6-ounces Neufchatel cheese
2 tablespoons canola oil, see note
3/4 cup natural sugar
1 teaspoon lemon extract
1 teaspoon lime juice
1 teaspoon lime zest

Place all ingredients in a blender or food processor container. Process until smooth; pour into ice cream freezer container. Freeze according to manufacturer's instructions. Makes 10 servings.

• Cook's note: Use canola oil only when this mixture is prepared with a non-dairy cream cheese substitute. Do not add oil when using Neufchatel cheese.

Nutritional information per serving:150.25 cal.; 6.08g total fat; 4.99g protein 19.80g carb.; 96.966mg sodium

Dietary Exchanges 1 bread; 0 fruit/vegetable; .6 protein; 1fat

MINTY CHUNKY-CHOCOLATE CREAM FREEZE

1/2 cup of natural semi-sweet chocolate bars, chopped
2 cups vanilla soymilk, rice milk or skim milk, chilled
1 teaspoon peppermint extract
1 (12.3-ounce) box firm silken tofu
6-ounces Neufchatel cheese
2 tablespoons canola oil, see note
3/4 cup natural sugar
2 tablespoons Dutch- processed cocoa
1 teaspoon vanilla extract

Begin melting chopped chocolate and peppermint in a saucepan over low heat. Remove from heat before chocolate completely melts. Stir off the heat to complete melting process. Set aside to cool. Combine remaining ingredients and process until smooth in a blender or food processor container. Pour into an ice cream freezer container and freeze according to manufacturer's instructions. Three to five minutes before freezing is complete; add melted chocolate to freezer container. Complete freezing process. Makes 11 servings.

• Cook's note: Use canola oil only when this mixture is prepared with a non-dairy cream cheese substitute. Do not add oil when using Neufchatel cheese.

Nutritional information per serving:165.12 cal.; 7.55g total fat; 5.62g protein 20.05g carb.;78.50mg sodium

Dietary Exchanges 1.2 bread; 0 fruit/vegetable; .5 protein; 1.2 fat

PISTACHIO FROZEN CREAM

2 cups vanilla soymilk, rice milk or skim milk, chilled
6-ounces non-dairy cream cheese substitute
or 1 (6-ounce) package Neufchatel cheese
1 (12.3-ounce) box firm silken tofu
2 tablespoons canola oil, see note
3/4 cup natural sugar
3/4 cup natural, chopped semi-sweet chocolate
1/2 cup natural creamy peanut butter
2 teaspoons vanilla extract

Place all ingredients in a blender jar. Process until smooth; pour into ice cream freezer container. Freeze according to manufacturer's instructions. Makes 11 servings.

- Cook's note: Use canola oil only when this mixture is prepared with a non-dairy cream cheese substitute. Do not add oil when using Neufchatel cheese.

Nutritional information per serving:163.19 cal.; 8.14g total fat;6.43g protein 17.11g carb.; 79.23mg sodium

Dietary Exchanges .9 bread; 0 fruit/vegetable; .7 protein; 1.5fat

PECAN SPICE DELIGHT CREAM

2 cups vanilla soymilk, rice milk or skim milk, chilled
6-ounces non-dairy cream cheese
or 1 (6-ounce) package Neufchatel cheese
2 tablespoons canola oil, see note
1 (12.3-ounce) box firm silken tofu
3/4 cup natural sugar
1 teaspoon vanilla extract
1 teaspoon vanilla butter nut extract
1/2 cup of pecans

Preheat oven to 350 degrees. Mix toasted pecans with 2 tablespoons of maple syrup. Toast for three to five minutes. Remove from oven. Let nuts come to room temperature before refrigerating.

Combine all other ingredients in a blender or food processor container. Process until smooth; pour into ice cream freezer container. Freeze according to manufacturer's instructions. Three to five minutes before freezing is complete, add chilled pecans to the freezer container. Complete freezing process. Makes 11 servings.

- Cook's note: To toast pecans: place crushed pecans on baking sheet and bake for one to three minutes, stirring occasionally.

- Cook's note: Use canola oil only when this mixture is prepared with a non-dairy cream cheese substitute. Do not add oil when using Neufchatel cheese.

Nutritional information per serving:170.32 cal.;8.76g total fat; 6.43g protein 18.56g carb.;77.08mg sodium

Dietary Exchanges 1 bread; 0 fruit/vegetable; .6 protein; 1.6 fat

REAL REESE CUP CREAM

2 cups vanilla soymilk, rice milk or skim milk, chilled
6-ounces non-dairy cream cheese substitute
or 1 (6-ounce) package Neufchatel cheese
1 (12.3-ounce) box firm silken tofu
2 tablespoons canola oil, see note
3/4 cup natural sugar
3/4 cup natural, chopped semi-sweet chocolate
1/2 cup natural creamy peanut butter
2 teaspoons vanilla extract

Begin melting chopped chocolate in a saucepan over low heat. Remove from heat before chocolate completely melts. Stir off the heat to complete melting process. Add peanut butter and mix well. Spread mixture on to wax paper and place in freezer for 10 to 15 minutes.

Remove wax paper from freezer (make certain chocolate is frozen); break into small chips. Set aside.

Place remaining ingredients in a blender or food processor container; process until smooth. Pour into an ice cream freezer container; freeze according to manufacturer's instructions. Three to five minutes before freezing cycle is complete, add chocolate and peanut butter chips to freezer container. Complete freezing process. Makes 13 servings.

- Cook's note: Use canola oil only when this mixture is prepared with a non-dairy cream cheese substitute. Do not add oil when using Neufchatel cheese.

Nutritional information per serving: 219.60 cal.;12.72g total fat;7.53g protein 21.79g carb.;116.45mg sodium

Dietary Exchanges 1.2 bread; 0 fruit/vegetable; .7 protein; 2.2fat

STRAWBERRY SUPREME CREAM

2 cups vanilla soymilk, rice milk or skim milk, chilled
6-ounces non-dairy cream cheese
or 1 (6-ounce) package Neufchatel cheese
2 tablespoons canola oil, see note
1 (12.3-ounce) box firm silken tofu
3/4 cup natural sugar
1 teaspoon vanilla extract
1 teaspoon strawberry extract
1/2 cup fresh or frozen unsweetened strawberries

Place all ingredients in a blender or food processor container. Process until smooth; pour into ice cream freezer container. Freeze according to manufacturer's instructions. Makes 11 servings.

- Cook's note: Use canola oil only when this mixture is prepared with a non-dairy cream cheese substitute. Do not add oil when using Neufchatel cheese.

Nutritional information per serving:137.19cal.; 4.82g total fat;4.66g protein 19.20g carb.;89.98mg sodium

Dietary Exchanges .9 bread; 0 fruit/vegetable; .5 protein; .8fat

TOASTY BLACK WALNUTS

1/2 cup crushed black walnuts
2 cups vanilla soymilk, rice milk or skim milk, chilled
1 tub non-dairy cream cheese
or 1 (6-ounce) package Neufchatel cheese
2 tablespoons canola oil, see note
3/4 cup natural sugar
2 teaspoons vanilla extract

Preheat oven to 350 degrees. Place crushed walnuts on baking sheet and toast three to five minutes. Remove from oven and let come to room temperature before refrigerating.

Place remaining ingredients in a blender or food processor container. Process until smooth; pour mixture into ice cream freezer container. Freeze according to manufacturer's instructions. Three to five minutes before freezing is complete, add chilled walnuts to freezer container. Complete freezing process. Makes 11 servings.

• Cook's note: Use Canola oil only when this mixture is prepared with a non-dairy cream cheese substitute. Do not add oil when using Neufchatel cheese.
Nutritional information per serving:174.19 cal.; 8.29g total fat; 6.20g protein 19.72g carb.;93.36mg sodium
Dietary Exchanges .9 bread; 0 fruit/vegetable; .7 protein; 1.6 fat

TRIPLE TREAT SUNDAY

2 cups vanilla soymilk, rice milk or skim milk, chilled
6-ounces non-dairy cream cheese substitute or 1 (6-ounce) package Neufchatel cheese
2 tablespoons canola oil, see note
3/4 cup natural sugar
1 teaspoon vanilla extract
1 teaspoon of strawberry extract
1/2 cup of mashed banana
1/2 cup fresh or frozen strawberries
2 ounces melted chocolate

Place first seven ingredients in a blender or food processor container. Process until smooth; pour into ice cream freezer container. Freeze according to manufacturer's instructions. Three to five minutes before freezing is complete, add mashed bananas, chopped strawberries, and chocolate. Complete freezing process. Makes 13 servings.

• Cook's note: Use Canola oil only when this mixture is prepared with a non-dairy cream cheese substitute. Do not add oil when using Neufchatel cheese.
Nutritional information per serving: 160 cal.; 7.51g total fat;4.18g protein 20.40g carb.;78.99mg sodium
Dietary Exchanges .9 bread; 0 fruit/vegetable; .5 protein; 1.2fat

it must be jelly...
'cause jam doesn't
shake like that

some of my best memories of days gone by are fruity-licious

We not only picked fruit to make fresh pies, but we also picked fruit for my mother to can in order to make jellies, jams and preserves. Fruit that was overly ripe was used for jellies, and fruit that was just ripe was used for preserves and jams.

My mother would save mason jars for months as she prepared for the canning season. She would sterilize her jars and pour in the hot fruit. Then she would leave the jars to cool before placing them in a cool, dark place for the winter. Sometimes my siblings and I would use the pear preserves to make a pear sandwich. My mother would serve preserves, jelly and jam with biscuits for breakfast. What a great way to start our morning!

My mother's preserves, jellies and jam recipes used three times the amount of sugar than what is used in "Naturally Yours Gourmet Desserts." Large amounts of sugar were used to preserve the fruit for up to one year. My recipes only require one third of the sugar from my mom's recipes, and they taste just as wonderful. However, they should not be refrigerated for more than one month.

GRANNY APPLE JELLY

Peelings from 6 medium apples
1 1/2 cups natural sugar
3 cups water
1 1/2 packages pectin,
each package weighs 1.75 ounces

Cover peelings with water and boil for one hour on low heat. Strain juice through cheesecloth until liquid is clear. Allow to set for five hours. Bring to another boil; use a slotted spoon to remove foam.

Reduce heat; stir in sugar and pectin. Continue stirring until mixture begins to gel. Makes one pint.

• Cook's note:: Jellies may be refrigerated for up to one month.

Nutritional information per 20g serving (equal to slightly more than a tablespoon): 18.64 cal.; 0g total fat; 0g protein 4.92g carb.; 1.35mg sodium

Dietary Exchanges .4 bread; 0 fruit/vegetable; 0 protein; 0 fat

PEAR JELLY

Peels and cores from 6 medium pears
1 1/2 natural cups sugar
3 cups water
1 1/2 package pectin, each package weighs
1.75 ounces

Cover peelings with water and boil for one hour on low heat. Strain juice through cheesecloth until liquid is clear. Allow to set for five hours. Bring to another boil; use a slotted spoon to remove foam.

Reduce heat; stir in sugar and pectin. Continue stirring until mixture begins to gel. Makes one pint.

• Cook's note:: Jellies may be refrigerated for up to one month.

Nutritional information per 20g serving (equal to slightly more than a tablespoon): 19.58 cal.; 0g total fat; 0g protein 5.10g carb.; 2.05 mg sodium

Dietary Exchanges .4 bread; 0 fruit/vegetable; 0 protein; 0 fat

BLACKBERRY JELLY

3 pounds frozen unsweetened blackberries
1 1/2 cups natural sugar
1 1/2 (1.75 ounce-packet) pectin

Thaw frozen blackberries. Crush berries and strain through a cheesecloth. Place juice in saucepan over low heat and add sugar. Stir well.

Increase heat until mixture comes to a boil. Remove foam. Boil on high heat for two minutes and stir in pectin. Continue to stir until mixture begins to gel. Pour jellied mixture into prepared sterilized jars and seal with lid. Makes four pints.

• Cook's note:: Jellies may be refrigerated for up to one month.

Nutritional information per 20g serving (equal to slightly more than a tablespoon): 26.21 cal.; 0g total fat; 0g protein 6.69g carb.; 1.91 mg sodium

Dietary Exchanges .4 bread; 0 fruit/vegetable; 0 protein; 0 fat

PEACH JELLY

Peels from 6 medium peaches
1 3/4 cups of natural sugar
3 cups of water
1 (1.75-ounce) packet of pectin

Cover peach peelings with water and boil for one hour on low heat. Strain juice through cheesecloth until liquid is clear. Allow to set for five hours. Bring to another boil; use a slotted spoon to remove foam.

Reduce heat; stir in sugar and pectin. Continue stirring until mixture begins to gel. Makes one pint.

• Cook's note: Jellies may be refrigerated for up to one month.

Nutritional information per 20g serving (equal to slightly more than a tablespoon): 21.45 cal.; 0g total fat; .06g protein 5.56g carb.; 1.56 mg sodium

Dietary Exchanges .4 bread; 0 fruit/vegetable; 0 protein; 0 fat

STRAWBERRY JELLY

3 pounds frozen unsweetened strawberries
1 1/2 cups natural sugar
1 1/2 package pectin, each package weighs 1.75 ounces

Crush berries and strain through a cheesecloth. Place juice in saucepan over low heat and add sugar. Stir well. Increase heat until mixture comes to a boil; use a slotted spoon to remove foam. Boil on high heat for two minutes; stir in pectin. Continue to stir until mixture begins to gel. Pour jellied mixture into prepared sterilized jars and seal with lid. Makes four pints.

• Cook's note: Jellies may be refrigerated for up to one month.

Nutritional information per g serving (equal to slightly more than a tablespoon): 21.66 cal.; 0g total fat; 0g protein 5.66g carb.; 2.07 mg sodium

Dietary Exchanges .4 bread; .0 fruit/vegetable; .0 protein; .0 fat

2 quarts of fresh or frozen strawberries
2 cups of natural sugar
3 tablespoons of lemon juice

If you are using fresh strawberries, soak, wash, and remove stems before using. Combine strawberries and natural sugar in large boiler. Place boiler on medium heat and allow mixture to cook for 15 minutes. Let stand for two or three hours. Bring to a boil and separate strawberries from juice. Boil juice until it thickens.

Pour juice over strawberries and allow them to set for two more hours. Bring to another boil and remove foam using a slotted spoon. Strawberries are ready to be ladled or poured into sterilized jars and sealed with metal lid. Makes five half-pints.

Nutritional information per g serving (equal to slightly more than a tablespoon): 24.14 cal.; 0g total fat; 0g protein 6.26g carb.; .35mg sodium

Dietary Exchanges. .4 bread; .0 fruit/vegetable; .0 protein; .0 fat

PEACH PRESERVES

Peels from 6 medium peaches
1 3/4 cups of natural sugar
1/2 cup water
1 (1.75-ounce)
packet of pectin

If you are using fresh peaches, wash, peel and quarter before using. Combine peaches and sugar in large boiler or Dutch oven. Cover and let stand for two hours.

Add water and cook on medium heat bringing peaches to a boil. Stir frequently so that peaches will not stick. Add lemon juice and return to a boil and cook for another 20 minutes or until peaches are soft. Remove foam with a metal slot spoon. Makes four half-pints.

Nutritional information per g serving (equal to slightly more than a tablespoon): 22.29 cal.; 0g total fat; 0g protein 5.76g carb.; .08mg sodium
Dietary Exchanges .4 bread; fruit/vegetable; protein; fat

PEAR PRESERVES

2 quarts fresh
or frozen peaches
2 cups natural sugar
3 cup water
3 tablespoons of lemon juice

If you are using fresh pears, wash, peel and quarter before using. Place pears in a large boiler and cover with water. Bring to a boil; cover pears and reduce heat and simmer for 15-18 minutes or until pears are soft. Remove from heat and drain. Add sugar to pears and bring to another boil. Cook on low heat for five minutes or until mixture thickens. Remove foam with a metal slot spoon.

Spoon hot pears into sterilized jars and seal with metal lids. Fills four half-pint jars.

Nutritional information per g serving (equal to slightly more than a tablespoon):18.81 cal.; 0g total fat; 0g protein 5.10 g carb.; 1.85 mg sodium
Dietary Exchanges .4 bread; fruit/vegetable; protein; fat

BLACKBERRY PRESERVES

2 quarts of fresh
or frozen blackberries
2 cups of natural sugar
3 tablespoons of lemon juice

If you are using fresh blackberries, soak, and wash before using. Combine blackberries and natural sugar in large boiler. Place boiler or Dutch oven on medium heat and allow mixture to cook for 15 minutes. Remove from heat and let it stand for two to three hours. Bring to a slow boil and remove foam with a slotted spoon. Remove from heat and spoon into prepared sterilized jars and seal with lid. Jars are to remain in a pan of boiling water.

Nutritional information per g serving (equal to slightly more than a tablespoon): 26.21 cal.; 0g total fat; 0g protein 6.69 g carb.; .20 mg sodium
Dietary Exchanges .3bread; fruit/vegetable; protein; fat

SPICY APPLE BUTTER

8 cored medium apples
1 cup natural unsweetened
concentrated apple juice
3/4 cup natural sugar
2 tablespoons lemon juice
1 teaspoon nutmeg
1 teaspoon cinnamon

Combine apples and 1 cup of apple juice and natural sugar in a large boiler or Dutch oven. Place top on boiler and cook on medium to low heat for 45 minutes or until apples are soft. Stir continuously so that apples do not stick. Drain and puree apples with food processor. Combine puree with lemon juice, nutmeg, and cinnamon. Return to medium heat and cook for 20 minutes or until mixture becomes thick. Remove from heat and use slotted spoon to skim off foam.

Pour apple mixture into prepared sterilized jars and seal with lid. Makes five pints.

Nutritional information per g serving (equal to slightly more than a tablespoon): 18.82 cal.; 0g total fat; 0g protein 4.97g carb.; 1.35 mg sodium
Dietary Exchanges .1 bread; fruit/vegetable; protein; fat

Mom's

MOM AND ME TOGETHER AGAIN... COOKING UP SOME GREAT DESSERTS.

This section is very special to me for many reasons. First of all, I am a mother. My husband and I are the proud parents of our handsome son, Denard. He was a beautiful baby who cried continuously from the day he was born until he was four weeks old. We finally realized he cried all of the time because he was allergic to milk. We tried several formulas with unsuccessful results. As a last resort, his pediatrician recommended soymilk. I prayed that this formula would work for him, and it did.

Denard's early years were very challenging for him and for us. I observed that whenever we visited his

Choice

grandmother's farm, he experienced a negative reaction to the fresh hen eggs. I soon learned that he was not only allergic to dairy but also to eggs and products made from corn. In addition to these concerns, he developed asthma.

As Denard grew, I learned more about how foods affected his asthma and allergies. I packed his lunch daily and would only include nutritional foods such as natural applesauce, raisins and turkey sandwiches on wheat bread. These foods did not cause an allergic reaction that normally would lead to an asthma attack. Since that time, I have learned that Denard was also allergic to wheat.

Denard could not drink milk or consume foods that contained red dye. Sometimes at school he would intentionally get chocolate milk, but the children would tell on him. The teacher solicited the other students' assistance to help her monitor students who had special diets.

Denard, for the most part, accepted his fate, and as I learned more about allergies and foods that impacted allergies, Denard's diet became very bland. He could not even have popcorn at the movies.

In our current society, no child should be deprived of cake and ice cream unless it presents a medical challenge. By removing everything from Denard's diet that would present a problem, I believed he would outgrow his childhood illnesses. Well, he did not outgrow these medical conditions, but I learned that I did not want to ruin his childhood or adolescence by always saying no. Although we have removed some foods that he and I both are allergic to, we have replaced them with foods that are just as good. Since my son and I are lactose intolerant, I replaced milk with soy, and I replaced wheat flour with oat and rice flour. He loves soy ice cream! I no longer have to worry that he will sneak to partake in any of those "no no" desserts.

That is the beginning of Mom's Choice. Children can still have their favorite cake, ice cream, smoothies and cookies. Desserts are not so harmful, but it is the ingredients used in the desserts that make the difference.

I am principal of an elementary school with 950 students. Many of the adults and students struggle with allergies, asthma,

diabetes and other diseases. After my family and I made a lifestyle change, I found that we were healthier and suffered from fewer illnesses. Two years ago, I created a nutritional team at my school and shared with them my idea to become a model school for good nutrition. They bought into it. The next job was to sell the idea to the parents. The parents loved the idea and supported me in helping their children make healthy lifestyle changes. We are probably one of the few schools in the state of Georgia that does not serve chocolate milk, punch drinks, nor desserts on a daily basis unless we modify the ingredients. I taught my students to read labels. They now bring fresh fruit, and we offer water and natural fruit juices as a beverage. We have also seen a marked improvement in our test scores. My students know that Dr. Butler just wants them to be healthy and happy.

The dessert recipes that have been included in the Mom's Choice section are recipes that you and your children can enjoy.

BAKED CINNAMON RAISIN APPLE (*A+APPLES*)

1 medium apple
1 tablespoon raisins
1/2 teaspoon ground cinnamon

Preheat oven to 350 degrees. Wrap washed apple in aluminum foil; bake for 20 minutes. Dust raisins with cinnamon; set aside. Unwrap apple cut in half; remove core. Replace core with raisin/cinnamon mixture. Return to oven. Bake 10 additional minutes. Let cool before serving. Makes one serving.

Nutritional information per serving: 135.39 cal.; 2.85 total grams fat; .64g protein 30.18g carb.; 1.54 mg. sodium

Dietary Exchanges 0 bread; 1.9 fruit/vegetable; 0 protein; .4 fat

PATTY WHACK STEWED PEAR

2 medium pears, peeled and cored
1/2 cup unsweetened apple cider
1 teaspoon sugar, optional
1/2 teaspoon ground cloves

Cut pears into quarters; place in saucepan. Cover with apple cider and optional sugar. Bring mixture to a boil and simmer for 15 minutes. Remove pears with slotted spoon. These are delicious served warm or cold. Makes two servings.

Nutritional information per serving: 130.92 cal.; 1.18 total grams fat; 1.07g protein 32.59g carb.; 3.2 mg. sodium

Dietary Exchanges 0 bread; 2.2 fruit/vegetable; 0 protein; 0 fat

GOOD OL' SWEET POTATO

1 large sweet potato
1 teaspoon canola oil
1 tablespoon unsweetened applesauce
1/2 teaspoon ground cinnamon

Heat oven to 375 degrees. Rub potato with oil; wrap in aluminum foil. Place potato on baking sheet and bake for 50 to 60 minutes. Remove potato from oven. Unwrap; cut in half. Dust potatoes with cinnamon and top each half with a dollop of applesauce. Serve warm or cold. Makes one serving.

Nutritional information per serving: 186.5 cal.;4.98 total grams fat; .2.22g protein 34.30g carb.; 17.54 mg. sodium

Dietary Exchanges 1.7bread; 0 fruit/vegetable; 0 protein; .9 fat

BANANA SPLIT POP

1 medium banana, peeled
1 ounce pre-melted semi-sweet natural chocolate
3 tablespoons crushed peanuts or pecans

Wrap banana in foil and freeze. Pour semi-sweet chocolate over banana. Roll chocolate covered banana into crushed nuts. Allow to set for several minutes before serving. Makes one serving.

Nutritional information per serving: 410.2 cal.; 1.18 total grams fat; 9.18g protein 32.59g carb.; 3.2mg. sodium

Dietary Exchanges 0 bread; 2.2 fruit/vegetable; 0 protein; 0 fat

BERRY BERRY SMOOTHIE

3/4 cup unflavored soymilk, chilled
1/4 cup plain low fat yogurt or non-dairy yogurt substitute
1/4 cup strawberry slices
1/4 cup blueberries
2 teaspoons natural sugar
1 teaspoon vanilla extract

Place ingredients in blender and blend to reach a smooth consistency. Makes two servings.

Nutritional information per serving: 101.29 cal.; 2.85 total grams fat; 4.63g protein 15.66g carbs.; 34.06 mg. sodium

Dietary Exchanges .4 bread; .5 fruit/vegetable; 0 protein; .4 fat

TROPICAL SMOOTHIE

3/4 cup unflavored soy milk, chilled
1/4 cup plain low fat yogurt or non-dairy yogurt
1 (8 ounce) can unsweetened crushed pineapples
1/4 cup frozen or fresh unsweetened coconut
2 teaspoons natural sugar
1 teaspoon coconut extract
1/2 teaspoon almond extract

Place ingredients in blender and blend to reach a smooth consistency. Makes two servings.

Nutritional information per serving: 166.49 cal.; 9.18 total grams fat;5.44g protein 17g carbs.; 37.33 mg. sodium
Dietary Exchanges .4 bread; .5 fruit/vegetable; 0 protein; 1.8 fat

BANANA GRANOLA SMOOTHIE

3/4 cup vanilla soymilk, chilled
1/4 cup plain low fat yogurt or non-dairy yogurt
1 small banana
1/2 cup natural granola crumbs
2 teaspoons natural sugar
1 teaspoon vanilla extract

Place ingredients in blender and blend to reach a smooth consistency. Makes two servings.

Nutritional information per serving: 283.83 cal.; 9.77total grams fat; 6.17g protein 44.95g carb.; 106.69mg. sodium
Dietary Exchanges 1.4 bread; .7 fruit/vegetable; 0 protein; 1.6 fat

STRAWBERRY & BANANA SMOOTHIE SUPREME

3/4 cup unflavored soymilk, chilled
1/2 cup plain low fat yogurt or non-dairy yogurt
1 small banana
1/2 unsweetened fresh or frozen strawberry slices
1 teaspoon vanilla extract

Place ingredients in blender and blend to reach a smooth consistency. Makes two servings.

Nutritional information per serving: 213.61 cal.; 13.61 total grams fat; 5.02g protein 19.53g carb.; 36.53mg. sodium
Dietary Exchanges 1bread; 1 fruit/vegetable; 0 protein; 2.6fat

APPLE BUTTER BASKETS

2 shells from a package pastry shells, made with unbleached white flour
2 tablespoons natural apple butter preserves
1/4 cup walnuts

Preheat oven to 400 degrees. Place pastry shell on baking sheet and place in oven for 20 minutes. Remove from oven. Make an indention in the center of each shell. Spoon one tablespoon of apple butter in the center of each shell; sprinkle with nuts. Makes two servings.

Nutritional information per serving: 338.0 cal.; 23.60 total grams fat; 5.7g protein 11.56g carb.; 5.42mg. sodium
Dietary Exchanges 2.3 bread; .6 fruit/vegetable; 0 protein; 4.2fat

COLOR ME KIDS GELATIN SQUIGGLES

4 envelopes unflavored
Emes Kosher-Jel or 4 envelopes unsweetened gelatin
1 cup organic fruit juice, chilled
3 cups organic fruit juice, heated
2 tablespoons natural sugar
1/2 chopped fresh or frozen fruit, no sugar added

Sprinkle gelatin substitute into a medium bowl; add cold juice. Remove from heat. Do not stir; let mixture rest for one minute. Stir in hot juice. Add gelatin and mix well. Blend in sugar. Add fruit. Pour into animal-shaped molds. Makes 12 shapes. Refrigerate until firm.

Nutritional information per serving: 56.6 cal.; .18 total grams fat; .2.65g protein 11.56g carb.; 5.42mg. sodium
Dietary Exchanges 0 bread; 1.9 fruit/vegetable; 0 protein; .4 fat

CARROT CAKE MUFFINS

2 1/2 cups unbleached all-purpose organic flour
1 1/2 cups natural sugar
2 teaspoons baking powder
1 teaspoon baking soda
2 teaspoons cinnamon
1 teaspoon salt (optional)
4 organic eggs
2 teaspoons vanilla extract
1/2 cup water
3/4 cup canola oil
3 cups grated carrots
1/2 cup crushed walnuts

Preheat oven to 375 degrees. Line muffin cups with paper liners; set aside. Sift together flour, baking powder, baking soda, cinnamon, sugar and salt; set aside.

Use a whisk to beat eggs until frothy. Blend in vanilla extract and water. Slowly pour in oil and whisk until mixture is well combined. Pour carrots and crushed nuts on top of sifted flour mixture; do not stir. Spoon egg mixture over flour and carrots. Use the whisk to blend ingredients into a smooth batter. Immediately spoon batter into prepared muffin cups. Bake for 20 minutes or until golden and muffins begin to pull away from the liners. Place pan on wire rack to cool for five to 10 minutes. Makes 12 to 14 muffins.

Nutritional information per serving: 498.14 cal.; total 26.57g fat; 10.18g protein 56.55g carb.; 445mg. sodium; Dietary Exchanges 3.1 bread; .60 fruit/vegetable; 1 protein; 4.7 fat

HEAVENLY CHOCOLATE MUFFINS

1 1/2 cups unbleached, all-purpose white flour
1 cup oat flour
1/2 cup Dutch-processed cocoa
1 1/2 teaspoons baking powder
1 teaspoon baking soda
1 tablespoon apple cider vinegar
2 teaspoons vanilla extract
1 teaspoon lemon extract
1 cup cold water
4 organic eggs
1 cup soy butter, cut in pats and melted in the microwave for approximately 35 seconds, see note
1 1/2 cups natural sugar
1/2 cup soymilk

Preheat oven to 350 degrees. Line muffin cups with paper liners; set aside. Flour needs to be sifted twice. Sift unbleached flour and oat flour together the first time. For the second sifting, combine flour, cocoa, sugar, baking powder, and baking soda; set aside. Whisk together milk, vinegar, vanilla extract, lemon extract, and water. Add eggs, one at a time, beating well after each addition. Add melted butter, whisking to blend well. Pour egg mixture over sifted dry ingredients. Use the whisk to blend ingredients into a smooth batter. Immediately spoon batter into prepared muffin tins. Bake for 20 minutes. Place the pan on wire rack to cool for five to 10 minutes. Makes 12 to 14 muffins.

Nutritional information per serving: 406.7 cal.; 11.62g total fat; 11.61g protein 64.13g carb.; 307mg. sodium;
Dietary Exchanges 3.2 bread; 0 fruit/vegetable; .8 protein; 1.7 fat
• Cook's note: after melting, leave soy butter inside closed microwave to keep it liquid.

HEAVENLY CHOCOLATE DAIRY-FREE MUFFINS

1 1/2 cups unbleached, all-purpose white flour
1 cup oat flour
1/2 cup Dutch-processed cocoa
1 1/2 cups natural sugar
1 teaspoon baking powder
2 teaspoons baking soda
2 tablespoons apple cider vinegar
2 teaspoons vanilla extract
1 teaspoon lemon extract
1 cup cold water
1 cup soy milk
1 cup soy butter, melted in microwave for approximately 30 seconds, see note

1/2 cup soy butter, melted in microwave for approximately 30 seconds, see note. Preheat oven to 375 degrees. Line muffin cups with paper liners; set aside. Sift flours twice. Sifting unbleached flour and oat flour together the first time. For the second sifting, combine flour, cocoa, sugar, baking powder, and baking soda; set aside. Whisk together milk, vinegar, vanilla extract, lemon extract, and water. Add melted butter, whisking to blend well. Pour vinegar/butter mixture over sifted dry ingredients. Use the whisk to blend ingredients into a smooth batter. Immediately spoon batter into prepared muffin tins. Bake for 20 minutes. Place pan on wire rack to cool for five to 10 minutes. Makes 12 to 14 muffins.

Nutritional information per serving: 287.41 cal.; 9.96 total grams fat; 4.57g protein 45.14g carb.; 150.68 mg. sodium
Dietary Exchanges 2.7 bread; 0 fruit/vegetable; 0 protein; 1.8 fat
• Cook's note: after melting, leave soy butter inside closed microwave to keep it liquid.

IT'S YOUR CHOICE

I hope that I have shared not only recipes that you can really enjoy but information that will be helpful to you in making a lifestyle change to help you live a healthier and happier life. It has taken me 25 years to make a lifestyle change that has made me mentally and physically stronger, so it is never too late.

I have always looked to others for the answers that only I had to make me happy. There will always be programs and plans that may give temporary success or happiness, but the only plan that will give you complete happiness is your plan. Yes, your plan. Many of the diets or programs in which I have been involved never empowered me. Instead, I became very dependent and fragile. Empowerment allows people to take control of their destiny.

There are programs and support groups that can assist you as you strive to reach your ultimate goal of a healthy lifestyle and weight loss. There are so many resources available to you. Guess what! Over 75 percent of the resources are free! I was convinced that if I did not pay several hundred dollars for a plan or a program to lose weight, it would not work for me.

If I could be reimbursed for some of the money that I spent on diet programs and plans, diet supplements, pills, exercise equipment, videos, and exercise programs, I would surely have saved a nice nest egg. I could probably pay a down payment for that cute new Lexus Sports car. You do the math. If you have been dieting for 10 years or more, and, in my case, 25 years, you could have spent from $3,000.00 to $60,000.00 dollars plus interest. When I realized how much I had paid while being unhappy, I could not believe it. I paid more than $45,000.00 for unhappiness and minimal weight loss. Do you know that over 50 million Americans go on some kind of diet each year? The percentage of success it is not great since over 60 percent of Americans are still overweight.

We make choices in life. Some choices we have to live with and some we do not. There will always be people who are looking for a miracle plan or program to help them fix their life; and there will always be people with a plan or program to help you fix your life. I would tell you to proceed with caution! It's your choice.

Five years ago when I hit rock bottom and had no place to go, I embarked on a journey that helped me take control of my life. For the first time I was not paying someone to tell me I could lose weight or work out a payment plan for me because I could not afford to pay those enormous fees. I had difficulty believing that something would finally work for me. I was afraid because I always had this written script from my previous programs.

Finally, I wrote my own script and plan. After many years I was able to do what no one else had done for me.

I am perceived to be a strong black female with several degrees, a modest home in the country, a handsome husband, a gifted son, and a designer wardrobe. What more could I possible need to make me happy? Whoever thought I would end up being in a support group!

I will tell you that if your lifestyle resembles mine in anyway, you will not be able to make your lifestyle change alone. There is help and hope. I joined a support group. It was one of the best choices that I have ever made in my life. They helped me to understand my compulsiveness and obsession with food and life. A support group is not a counseling program, rather it provides support and resources to help individuals make the best decisions for their health and food life.

Because I have been so supremely blessed, I want to help others who may be suffering. I began to research and hold seminars to better inform family, friends, and co-workers about what worked for me. I hold a group seminar once a week with many participants who I believe can testify that they too did not think that they could change the way that they have eaten all of their lives. But by the grace of God, they are making a successful lifestyle change.

Remember, changing your diet will not be enough to sustain you through this process. Your spiritual awareness and your physical program are major components to be taken seriously.

I am presently conducting personal consultations, and workshops for churches and businesses to help support more people in their quest for better health. I wish you well as you embark upon your healthier lifestyle change today.

NATURALLY YOURS TIPS FOR SUCCESS

- *Eat three well-balanced meals daily.*

- *Avoid snacking.*

- *Drink 8-10 glasses of water daily.*

- *Read literature to support your healthy lifestyle change.*

- *Read labels thoroughly on the back of food products.*

- *Exercise at least 30 minutes daily.*

- *Write in your journals each day.*

- *Take "before and after" pictures.*

- *Share your new lifestyle with everyone!*

INGREDIENTS & MORE

NATURAL INGREDIENTS

As I started making a lifestyle change to improve my health, I began to look at the foods that I prepared, especially desserts, and the ingredients that I used to prepare them. Changing the ingredients I used to make family desserts was a challenge for me. Many of my dessert recipes had been passed down from generation to generation. Even the slightest change of ingredients could destroy several lifetimes of work. How could I be true to my mother and all of my ancestors if I attempted to replace the traditional ingredients I had become so accustomed to using in my cakes and pies?

At first I decided to remove desserts from my diet altogether, and I did for over a year. It was a great thought, but was it realistic? I knew that if I were to be successful in making a healthy lifestyle change, I would have to find ways to modify my desserts.

I began to do extensive research on how natural ingredients benefitted our health and how I could prepare desserts with natural ingredients. I read much literature that was related to healthy cooking. I also subscribed to many health magazines and frequented grocery and health food stores that carried natural and organic ingredients for cooking and baking. Shortly thereafter, I began to experiment with some of the ingredients to make desserts that were suggested in the literature.

As I began to modify my recipes, I did not immediately replace all of the ingredients. I prioritized the ingredients and their significance to the recipe. I then modified one ingredient at a time for each recipe so that I would be able to determine how it affected the recipe. Each time I made the recipe, I added another natural ingredient. I continued this process until I had utilized each ingredient that would complete the recipe. This process afforded me an opportunity to determine which ingredients worked or did not work for me. This was quite an education.

At an early age, my mother taught me how to select my fruit for pies, jellies, jams and preserves. She also taught me how to select the best cake flours, butter and extract to make delicious cakes and pies. I used this same technique to select natural ingredients to modify and create natural desserts. When selecting fruit for pies, always look for fresh fruit that is not too ripe or bruised. The riper the fruit, the better it is for making jellies and jams. Ripe fruits have more natural juice which is excellent for preparing jelly and jam.

As I continued to modify traditional desserts and create my own healthy desserts using natural ingredients, I began to test them on family and friends. They could not believe that the desserts had been made using natural sugars, flours, butter and oil. They wanted to follow me home to see how I made these recipes, and, oftentimes, they did. It was then that I knew that I had found the missing link to making a healthy lifestyle change.

84

NATURAL SWEETENERS

According to the latest research, the average American consumes as much as two pounds of sugar a week. Many health experts believe that the amount of sugar we consume is directly related to obesity and health-related problems that occur in record numbers in the United States.

Before starting this wellness journey, I was unaware of how much sugar I consumed each day. After extensive research, I realized that sugar is not only in the desserts that we buy or prepare, but it is also in almost everything that we eat. Sugar is in natural fruit, even grains and vegetables. I was astonished when I learned how much sugar was in breakfast cereal. French fries, sodas, and also canned foods contain high percentages of sugar. When I was dieting, I used artificial sweeteners to reduce my sugar intake. I purchased diet sodas and desserts; however, I did not realize that artificial sugars also contained sugar.

If someone had told me that I would substitute natural sweeteners for white sugar to prepare my dessert recipes, I would have thought they were insane. Well, I now modify my dessert recipes with natural sweeteners and enjoy every minute of it.

TELL ME MORE ABOUT NATURAL SWEETENERS

Natural sweeteners are alternatives to white and refined sugars. When natural sweeteners are used, one reduces the sugar in most recipes by a third and sometimes even by a half. Unlike white sugar, natural sweeteners have no additives or preservatives. This is beneficial to one's health.

Many natural sweeteners are used in desserts. After modifying many of my dessert recipes with natural sweeteners, I found that several natural sweeteners worked best for me. Most of my recipes require dry (granulated) sweeteners such as natural Turbinado sugar, maple sugar and organic sugar. Liquid sweeteners such as maple syrup, unsulphured molasses and natural sugar-free fruit juice also work well in suggested recipes. I would not suggest the use of liquid sweeteners as a substitute for dry sweeteners unless specified in the recipe. I have found that some liquid natural sweeteners, although healthy, can be high in calories. I have not listed honey because honey works just like white sugar does in my body. It causes me to crave other sugars and carbohydrates, and it is sweeter than white sugar.

I use natural and frozen fruits in many of my recipes. I only use frozen fruits that contain no preservatives or added sugars. Fruits, as you know, are very healthy and are naturally sweetened by their own juices. I add only small amounts of natural sweeteners because they are necessary to create wonderful recipes. Various brands of sweeteners or sugars can be found in your local grocery stores. As you begin to cook with them, you will decide which ones you like best.

NATURAL INGREDIENTS

WHAT A DIFFERENCE FLOUR CAN MAKE

When I was a child, my mother never used cake flour. She always used all-purpose white and self-rising white flour. Until four years ago, I never used any other flours. Oh! I did cheat a little bit. I used cake flour for selected cakes, but don't tell my mother. I would have never imagined making a cake without white flour.

Education is priceless. Unbleached white flours and grain flours retain much of their original vitamins and minerals and are not as refined as regular white flours. This results in more fiber in our diets. Well, I do not use all-purpose white flour or cake flour in my recipes. I do use organic white flour, which is organically grown without any added chemicals. It is a wheat flour which has been carefully milled into white flour for baking purposes. Unbleached all-purpose white flour is a wheat flour that is milled into a soft fine flour and does not contain added chemicals. Self-rising unbleached white flour is made from soft red wheat with salt and aluminum-free baking powder added. Do not add additional salt, baking powder or baking soda when using self-rising flour. I do not suggest that you combine self-rising and unbleached white flours with other flours. Only use it in recipes that specify white flour. Whole grain flour, like whole-wheat pastry flour, is made from very soft wheat and milled into a very fine flour. The oak flour is milled from oak. Last, but not least, is soy flour, which is produced from the highest quality of soybeans. I only use soy flour in recipes that are strong in flavor like my chocolate cake, black cake or fruit cake. I do not recommend using soy flour in plain cakes, pies or muffins. I suggest that you sift your flour, especially whole grain flour, as you add it to the ingredients, unless the recipe specifies otherwise. Do not substitute whole-wheat flour for whole-wheat pastry flour. Your cake will be more like dry bread. Keep flour in the refrigerator in an air- tight container to ensure that freshness is maintained.

Master dessert makers who taught me most of what I know about baking never measured ingredients with traditional measuring utensils. Measuring has probably been the most difficult task for me to master throughout this book. However, for accuracy, one must measure ingredients to obtain the best results.

DAIRY ALTERNATIVES

MILK AND BUTTER

I could never have imagined life without ice cream, butter, cream cheese or milk. For a long time I did not know I was lactose intolerant to dairy products. No matter how bloated I became after eating ice cream or cheese, the taste was better than the misery that followed, or so I thought.

There are many people who believe that if their diet does not include dairy products, their bodies will not receive the required amounts of protein, vitamin D and calcium. The flip side of the coin is that many foods tend to be high in saturated fatty acids, which doctors say increase our risk of cancer.

Guess what? There are some great dairy alternatives. Yes, I know you are saying that you have tried some of those dairy alternatives like rice milk, soymilk, soy cream and butter, and they just do not taste as good as the dairy products. Well, those were my exact thoughts until I started to experiment with different brands and began using soy products as I modified recipes to make my delectable desserts. Dairy-free milk substitutes can be found in most of your local grocery stores, and many different brands are available. I know that you feel that only dairy butter will make your favorite dessert recipe. In many of my recipes I use oil, but for those recipes that only a good butter or margarine will do, I use non-dairy margarines and butter made from soybeans.

I have read many health magazines and books about soy products, and I have learned how soy helps to prevent diseases such as breast cancer, heart disease, hypertension, arthritis, diabetes, and osteoporosis. Since I suffer from several of these diseases, I have seen a marked improvement as I utilize soy products in my daily diet. I do believe that soy promotes overall health since it is low in fat and high in nutrients and fiber. Research also shows that soy can be helpful in the fight against obesity. So, what do we have to lose?

EGGS

I know what you are thinking. Yes, eggs are with the dairy products in the grocery store, but eggs are not dairy. The majority of my recipes are dairy-free, but all of them can be modified to be dairy-free. I have several recipes that are eggless. I am so eggcited. I can thank my friends who have chosen a vegetarian vegan lifestyle, which consists of no meat, eggs or dairy. I use organic eggs or eggs from free-range hens that are produced without the use of hormones and pesticides. I also use egg substitutes when feasible. However, eggs substitutes will not work for all recipes. When a cake recipe requires more than four eggs, the egg substitutes do not yield the desired results. They are excellent for cookies, fruit breads and puddings.

TOFU

Tofu is also produced from soybeans. I was introduced to tofu before I began my new healthy lifestyle journey. However, I had not used it as a dessert. As I shared with you earlier, I have many friends who are vegetarians, and they substituted tofu in many of their meat and dessert recipes. Now I use tofu in all of my ice creams. It gives the mixture a light smooth creamy texture.

Tofu is found in your local grocery store. There is shelf tofu and refrigerated tofu. Tofu is produced in silken, soft, medium firm and extra firm textures. I use firm regular and low fat tofu in my ice cream recipes. It is an excellent non-dairy ingredient.

FATS (BUTTER, MARGARINE, VEGETABLE SHORTENING AND OIL)

I used to hear the word fat and just cringe. When fat-free and low fat desserts hit the market, I knew I was home free. I bought every fat free product that was made. Several years ago I learned that most fat-free recipes required two to three times the amount of sugar as regular recipes. In several recipes I used low fat products, but I reduced the amount of sugar to yield the best results.

I believe that when we choose the highest quality of fats, we use the best quality for our recipes. I use non-dairy butter, margarine, canola oil and vegetable shortening. I love variety, and I think each recipe I prepare has a life of its own. Therefore, I select the fat that will yield the best flavor and results. I reduced the amount of fat that many of my traditional recipes require, and I have used only minimum amounts of fat in desserts I have created. Too much of any ingredient, regardless of its health benefit, can be harmful. When I was dieting, I thought because a recipe was low in sugar and considered low fat, I could eat twice as much. Well, I soon realized that I gained weight instead of losing it.

CHOCOLATES AND CAROB

Some say chocolate was the beginning of sin, but I believe that it was the making of heaven. Regardless of your thoughts on chocolates, I would suggest that you proceed with caution and enjoy them. When I use chocolate in my recipes, I use unsweetened chocolates, natural semi-sweetened chocolate or unsweetened dutch-processed cocoa.

People who refrain from chocolate use carob as a substitute for chocolate. Carob, like chocolate, comes from the pod of a tropical tree and is processed for use like chocolate. Carob has natural sugar, hydrogenated oil and dairy. I have eaten carob desserts, but I have not replaced carob with chocolate in my recipes. However, I will never say never.

SUBSTITUTIONS AND OTHER PERTINENT INFORMATION

Baking powder or baking soda is used in all recipes except when self-rising flour is suggested. I only use the Aluminum-free brand of baking powder, but you may use any brand that you find works for you.

I do not use regular salt. I only use iodized sea salt in my recipes. I use cornstarch and arrowroot instead of flour in pies or puddings. I always use soy milk instead of dairy milk. I make my own buttermilk. It is really easy. Just add 2 teaspoons of vinegar or lemon juice to one cup of soymilk. That's it. I have replaced all white sugars with unrefined natural sweeteners. I use natural and regular extract instead of imitation flavor in all of my recipes. You can also use non-alcoholic extracts.

When I am making dairy-free recipes that require gelatin, I use kosher gelatin. I also use an unsweetened brand name gelatin in many of my recipes. I only use organic cookies and crackers when they are required in a recipe. Be very careful when you are selecting your ingredients.

When a recipe requires peanut butter, please make sure that it is natural with no added sugar. Also, unsweetened applesauce is excellent and can be used to reduce oil in recipes. Proceed with caution. Only unsweetened coconut flakes are used in my recipes. I also use dried unsweetened coconut and frozen fresh unsweetened coconut.

I grew up eating white rice and sugar. I use brown basmati rice to make rice pudding. However, there are some brands of white rice that are excellent substitutes for rice pudding. If you are more comfortable with white rice, look in the health food department of your grocery store to select the best brand.

Many brand names are cashing in on the all-natural health food titles. When purchasing your ingredients, please read your labels carefully. Also, all sugars are not natural sugars. Brown sugar is not a natural sugar. It is the same as white sugar except for color. Read the fine print until you are comfortable with purchasing your ingredients.

If you do not find the ingredients you need, consult with your store manager. Many store managers will order the products for you.

NUTRITIONAL FACTS

THE WOMEN OF MY BAKING CIRCLE
WOULD MAKE THE GREATEST SACRIFICE OF ALL.

Many people I greatly admired as a child and who taught me everything I know about cooking are not here to see this book become a reality. These are women who never used a recipe and made flawless desserts. They spent countless hours in the kitchen just to make a recipe that would bring joy to their family, friends, or employers.

One night when I was having a problem with one of my recipes, I decided to call my cousin Christina who was known as the queen of desserts. She was a beautiful robust woman, inside and out. Chris, as we called her, lived in New Orleans and cooked for many prominent people in the city of New Orleans. During the holidays, it was impossible to move around in her small house. She had so many orders for carrot cake, red velvet cake and chess pies, that every tabletop dresser and chest was filled with her wonderful cakes. Tears just ran down my face when I thought about Chris passing some years earlier from cancer. I am convinced that her cancer had something to do with her being overweight, and that she did little or no exercise, and had a diet that was very rich in calories. The last memory I have of her before she left this world was icing a carrot cake for a young man she was nanny to as a child. It was the last glint of excitement I saw in her eyes. Several weeks after that, she was gone.

For Chris and all of my aunts, friends, and those of you who have lost loves ones from cancer, I have worked extremely hard to create and modify recipes so that they will be beneficial to our health. I have used ingredients that have not been over processed or stripped of the fiber and nutrients. I have researched every ingredient that I use to ensure that I have maintained the highest nutritional integrity for my recipes.

Soy milks and tofu are used in almost every recipe in this cookbook. Research has shown that they help prevent and treat illnesses, such as cancer, heart disease, hypertension, pre-menstrual syndrome, arthritis, diabetes and obesity.

In "Naturally Yours Gourmet Desserts," I have placed one of my many childhood favorite recipes, molasses bread, also known as molasses pudding. As a child, " Ms Earline" was like a second mother to me. She gave picking cotton in 105-degree temperatures dignity as she would bring our dinner to the field in large tin pans wrapped in white towels. She was one of my heroines, an excellent cook. She always had fresh churned, chilled, buttermilk, a large pan of molasses bread, pound cake, fried chicken and a lot of other "real good stuff." When I was writing the recipe for molasses bread, I called her to make sure that I had mixed the ingredients properly. She said." Baby, you know I suffer from diabetes, and the doctor told me that I could no longer have a lot of sugar so I just quit baking cakes and stuff. I just have some cookies from the store every now and then." I was a little saddened when she first told me, but she chuckled, and I felt better as we ended our conversation. I cannot wait to visit her and tell her that I have modified her molasses bread recipe. Therefore, she can still eat many of the desserts she is known for making throughout the county with her doctors' approval.

I have so many family, friends, group members and students who suffer from Type I diabetes. Type I diabetes is called the juvenile onset of diabetes. It has increased over the past three years as more families eat out and have diets that are high in carbohydrates. As a principal of an elementary school, I have seen more cases occur in young children. Type II diabetes is the adult-onset of diabetes, and it occurs in the majority of people who experience diabetes and are overweight. The third type of diabetes is called gestational diabetes and can occur during pregnancy.

I know that oftentimes diabetics crave desserts and partake of desserts that are not condusive to improving their health. In my recipe book, I have analyzed all of the recipes so that diabetics are provided with healthy selections and do not need to feel they have to sneak and eat desserts that will result in health complications. I am not a physician so I recommend consulting with your doctor.

Ms. Lorine Bizzell, a registered dietitian and certified nutritionist, has performed the analysis for "Naturally Yours Gourmet Desserts" nutritional charts, which include diabetic exchanges. She has utilized the Food Processor produced by ESHA Research.

Please be aware of the following as you select dessert recipes that are best for you.

Use the nutritional chart as a guide and not as a prescription. The ingredients listed first have been analyzed, using the optional ingredients could change the value of the ingredients.

NUTRITIONAL NOTES

TIPS FOR SELECTING YOUR FAVORITE DESSERTS

I no longer eat desserts everyday. However, there are times when I am creating recipes or getting ready for a cooking display, and I will prepare 15 to 20 desserts over several days. I have to test each of them. I prepare for those instances a little differently than when preparing more than two desserts. I normally begin the morning with warm lemon water or lemon zinger tea. I squeeze the juice of half a lemon into a cup and pour warm water until the cup is three-quarters full. After my lemon with water or tea, I eat half a red grapefruit or a citrus fruit. I have lots of green raw and cooked vegetables along with protein and plenty of water. Water helps to cleanse and revitalize the body.

I have learned that whether you are serving one or two desserts with a meal, you must consider the entire menu from the appetizer to the dessert. When I am serving a chocolate cake, I will not include potato salad or macaroni and cheese. I will choose cooked and raw vegetables with this dessert. The chocolate cake, although delicious and made with natural ingredients, is very rich. If I were going to prepare a meal with starches such as potato salad or pasta, I would prepare a very light dessert such as soy ice cream, pie, or a selection from Mom's choice. Unbaked desserts and fresh fruit are always options when a quick and delicious dessert is needed.

You cannot live on desserts alone. I have tried that too, and it just does not work. When you prepare your meals, make an extra effort to select foods from every food group. I worked very hard to select foods that would give me the maximum health benefit. Also, increase your green and yellow vegetable intake. Ever had a day when you prepared several desserts before you settled on one? Well, those are days you might want to choose fruit. It is simple but tasty and quite healthy and it will save you calories, if you're counting.

Rich desserts should not only be eaten with plenty of green vegetables, but the earlier in the day you eat them, the better. The time of the day you eat desserts can impact your food plan significantly. I have desserts that I eat for breakfast like rice pudding or bread pudding. I eat desserts that are richer and higher in calories at lunch. I save lighter desserts for dinner. If you choose to eat desserts in the afternoon, opt for lighter desserts and fresh fruit. As you begin to prepare and enjoy your healthy selections, you will determine what works best for you and your body since no one knows your body better than you.

To GOD be the glory! Because of You I am and because of You I will always be blessed

First of all, to my mom, Mrs. Ruth Sanders, I want to thank you for holding my hand at age four to help me make cookie dough. I want to thank you for holding my hand today while I modified the family jelly and preserve recipes, and I want to thank you for assuring me that all of the recipes in "Naturally Yours Gourmet Desserts" were perfect. Mom, you have always believed in me and loved me. I dedicate this cookbook to you and to all mothers, and to Mrs. Lillian & the late Mr. Vernon Lynch Sr. for inspiring me to make a nutritional difference in the lives of others.

To my Daddy Bo, West Sanders, you will always be my hero. Your love and support will always sustain me. I will always love you daddy.

To my dearest husband, Floyd whom I have loved since I was thirteen. At 44, I love you even more. To my loving son, Denard, my cowboy. Life has great things in store for you. Always put God first and everything else you want or need will follow.

To my six beautiful sisters, the fantastic six, Dorothy(Dot), Lillie(Jim), Shirley(Shelley), Doris(Mick), Betty, and Annette(Wanky), you have always supported me in all of my endeavors without reservation. You girls are the greatest, and I love you. To all of my brother-in-laws, especially Roosevelt, Fulton, Thaddeus, Mack, Kenny for your unconditional love and support. And to Johnnie I will always remember you being there for me in the early years when I needed you the most. To my sister-in-laws, especially Hazel, Sadie(my girl) and Zerlene for all of your support. To my nieces and nephews, especially my "Lil" Star and Brady Boy, remember age is nothing but a number. Live your life to the fullest and never quit dreaming. What would life be without your best girlfriend? I love you Rose " Danny" Johnson. To the girls who I could not love more if I had given birth to them, Anjulia and Simone. The world has great things in store for you. You are the greatest! Luke, God has given my parents a son and us a brother. You are a testament of God's love and grace.

I would be remiss if I did not give a special thanks to these very unique ladies whom I call the "Naturally Yours Faith-Based Team." I could not have done it without you. A very special thank you goes out to Hazel Lucas, Tanyetta Goodjiones, Alfreda Trawick and Sadie Butler for always making the connection and the deadlines. Special Kudos to Ms. Joanne Cooper, Ife Green, Judy Khan, and Frenchella Thibedeaux. Thanks to the talented and gifted P. N. K., my angel, for his creative support.

94

No project is successful without the love and support of great friends and colleagues.

Jemel and Marie, I would like to thank you for all of your love, support and your encouragement through this process. You are the greatest. Thank you Mae for your love and prayers throughout this entire process. Thanks to my adopted brothers, Lonzo & Lonnie, for not letting me stop even when I wanted to, and to my very special brothers and friends Mike Glenn and Curtis Bunn who have successfully chartered the waters before me. Your support and care during this process have meant so much to me.

To the Browns Mill faculty, staff, parents, and students, I appreciate you for all of your support and love. You are the true meaning of family. I also would like to thank you for testing all of my recipes.

Thanks to Jeanette Patton, the mother and manager of the talented R&B artist "Usher", for opening her beautiful home to the crew and me to do all of the personal photos in the cookbook. She is not only a gracious host but also a dynamic lady.

Thanks to two of my very special friends, Lamar Williams and Audrey Williams, for allowing the crew and me to take over their lovely countryside home for two days to shoot the layout for the delicious recipes. Thanks to Earl Thomas and Pamella Thomas of RMT Construction Inc. for opening their beautiful and exquisite home to me for yet another photo shoot. Mr. Thomas, your success as one of the greatest builders of luxury homes for the rich and famous has not caused you to lose your compassion for mankind.

Thanks to Herman Cunningham and Vernessa Cunningham for not only opening your beautiful home to me so that I could complete my photos for the cookbook, but also for supporting Floyd and me with your love and prayers throughout this entire process. You both have a very special place in my heart.

Thanks to Ms. Shannon Mocyk, Denard's counselor at Stockbridge High School, who has gone beyond the call of duty to support and advise our son during his senior year and made sure that he pursued all of the educational opportunities that were available to him.

Thank you Ms. Nellie Lewis for the creation and design of my chef jacket. Great Job! Thank you Mike Hall for consulting with me on my vegetarian dessert recipes. You are the greatest.

95

INDEX

INDEX

JOURNAL

JOURNAL

JOURNAL

JOURNAL

JOURNAL

JOURNAL

JOURNAL

JOURNAL

JOURNAL

RESOURCES

1. American Natural Snacks
St. Augustine, FL 32085
MI-Del Cookies

2. Arrowhead Mills–Arrowhead Mills,
Inc.
Box 2059
Hereford, TX 79045
1-800-364-0730
Pastry flour
Stone ground flour
All Purpose Baking Mix

3. Better Than Milk
Division of Fuller Life Inc.
1628 Robert C. Jackson Drive
Maryville, TN 37801
1-800-227-2320
Vegan Beverage Mix
Better Than Milk

4. Bob's Red Mill Natural Food Line
5209 S. E. International Way
Milwaukee, OR 97222
1-503-654-3215
Whole Wheat Flour
Unbleached Flour

5. Country Choice Nature
P. O. Box 44247
Minneapolis, MN 55349
Country Choice Vanilla Wafers

6. Delicious Brands, Inc.
2070 Maple Street
Des Plaines, IL 60018 USA
Frookie (All Natural Wafer)

7. Ener-g Foods Inc.
1-800-331-5222
www.ener-g.com
Egg Replacer

8. Fearn Natural Foods
Division of Modern Products, Inc.
Milwaukee, WI 53029
Fearn Naturally Flavored Cake Mix

9. Florida Crystal
www.FloridaCrystal.com
Natural Sugar-Milled Cane

10. Haines Pure Food
1-800-434-4246
Turbinado Sugar (All Purpose Natural
Sweetener)
Sallflower Oil Margarine

11. King Flour Company
Box 1010
Norwich, VT 05055
www.KingArthur.Flour.com
King Arthur Flour
Unbleached All Purpose Flour
Unbleached Special Bread Flour

12. Morinaga Nutritional Food, Inc.
2050 W. 190th St., 110
Torrance, CA 90504
www.Morinu.com
Silken Tofu

13. Tofutti Brands Inc.
Cranford, NJ
1-800-956-6624
Tofutti Better Than Cream Cheese

14. Surf White Wave
www.SilkIsSoy.com
White Wave Silk Milk

15. Whole Foods Market
For a list of locations nationwide, contact their corporate headquarters in Austin, TX
1-512-477-4455

16. Wild Oats Market
For a list of locations nationwide, contact their hotline at1-800-494-WILD or www.wildoats.com

NATURALLY YOURS
BIBLIOGRAPHY

Appleton, N. (Ph.D). (1996). Lick the sugar habit. Garden City Park, NY. Avery Publishing Group.

Better Homes and Gardens (1988). Meredith Publishing Group. Des Moines, IA.

Buhr, D. (1997). The "I can't believe this has no sugar" cookbook. New York, NY. St. Martin Griffin.

Costigan, F. (1999). Great good desserts. New York, NY. Good Cakes Production.

Diabetes Forecast (March 2002). American Diabetes Association. Vol. 55. No. 3. Alexandria, VA.

Diabetic Cooking (May/June 2002). Publications International, Ltd.

Dufty, W. (1976). Sugar blues. New York, NY. Warner Books Inc.

Gaines, F. D., & Weaver, R. (1999). The new soul food cookbook for people with diabetes. American Diabetes Association. Alexandria, VA.

Goodman, D. G. (1999). Somethin' to shout about! Stone Mountain, GA. Orion Enterprise.

Hamilton, E. M., Whitney, E., & Sizer, F. (1988). Nutrition concept & controversies. (4th ed.). New York. West Publishing Company.

Holt, S. (M. D.) (1998). The soy revolution. New York, NY. Dell Publishing.

Jenson, B. (Ph. D.) (2000). Guide to natural weight control. Los Angeles, CA.

Keats Publishing.

Lobue, A., & Marsea, M. (1999). The don't diet live-it workbook. Carlsbad, CA.

Meyer, J. (2000). Eat and stay thin. Tulsa, OK. Harrison House, Inc.

Gurze Books.

Sheppard, K. (1989). Food addiction the body knows. Dearfield Beach, FL.

Health Communications, Inc.

The southern living cookbook. (1987). Birmingham, AL. Oxmoor House, Inc.

Williams, J., & Silverman, G. (1993). No salt, no sugar, no fat. San Leandro, CA. Briston Publishing Enterprises.

NATURALLY YOURS
CONTACT & ORDERING INFORMATION

Naturally Yours & More Inc.
Voicemail : 770-322-1832
e-mail:Naturallyyours@ybnatural.com
Address: Naturally Yours and More
P.O Box 892
Ellenwood, Georgia. 30294
www.ybnatural.com

Photographer	Designer	Stylist	Hair Stylist	Make up Artist
Terence Li	Michael Angelo Chester	Jay Lee	Dorothy Rose of	Cheryl Thomas
www.bellowsfactor.com	macpress57@hotmail.com	Photovirus@yahoo.Com	Hairspot Salon	Cheryl@earthlink.net
404-578-7574	770-416-9316	678-557-8263	404-589-9801	770-368-7180
			dorothyrose@email.com	

Dr. Yvonne Sanders-Butler is a wife, mother, educator, and a self-taught chef who specializes in Naturally prepared Gourmet Desserts. She has been cooking since the age of four. While most of her childhood friends were playing with dolls, she stood in a chair at the kitchen table stirring cake batter, rolling cookie dough, and sampling icing for cake. When she was not cooking with her mother, she was seeking secrets of the best-known cooks in the community.

Since those early years of cooking bliss, she encountered several major health concerns that would have certainly removed desserts from her cooking repertoire. What would life be without her famous Butter Pound Cake, Sweet Potato Cobbler, and Heavenly Chocolate Caramel Cake?

Instead of giving up one of her greatest joys in life-cooking and preparing desserts, Yvonne began modifying many of traditional southern dessert recipes and began creating her own desserts by using natural ingredients. Not only were the desserts delicious and satisfying, but the health benefits were phenomenal. She lost five dress sizes without dieting in the process.

In her first book of natural dessert recipes, Yvonne includes some of her most tasty treats. Best of all you can still enjoy delectable desserts without worrying about extra weight gain or about our health.

110